WELFARE ECONOMIC THEORY

WELFARE ECONOMIC THEORY

JOHN F. O'CONNELL
College of the Holy Cross

 Auburn House Publishing Company
Boston, Massachusetts

Library of Congress Cataloging in Publication Data

O'Connell, John Frederick, 1942–
  Welfare economic theory.

  Includes index.
  1. Welfare economics.   I. Title.
HB846.026   330.15′5   82-1760
ISBN 0-86569-087-1   AACR2

Printed in the United States of America

To my mother and
the memory of my father

PREFACE

The purpose of this book is to introduce to students, with relatively little mathematical training and only the usual intermediate economic theory course (more particularly at the microlevel), many of the topics at the frontier of economics. Given the growing general interest in economics and its increasingly scientific nature, the gap between undergraduate and graduate courses has grown larger and larger. Bridging this gap requires that undergraduate theory courses be more analytical and rigorous in fundamentals, often at the expense of those topics that preoccupy advanced discussions. Externalities, general equilibrium, public goods, income distribution, and dynamic optimization—all of which dominate learned journals—can be treated only superficially at the undergraduate level. We try here to introduce these topics in a detailed yet intuitive way to those not having advanced training, thus providing a vehicle for bridging the expanse between the nucleus of economics and the frontier.

I have used much of this material in a course taught to advanced undergraduates entitled Welfare Economics. The text could be equally well used in a first-year graduate course in microeconomic theory with a policy orientation. Large parts would also be applicable to courses in public finance and to anyone involved in the general area of economic policy making. Conceptually, more difficult topics are presented in a number of different ways: verbally, algebraically, and graphically. Efforts are made not to be overly compromising in the rigor of the discussion, yet the arguments rely heavily on intuitive reasoning. A rather elementary knowledge of calculus is assumed although the use of advanced mathematics is avoided.

After introducing the topic of welfare economics in Chapter 1, we develop optimizing conditions under the simplest (purely competitive, comparative static) assumptions in Chapter 2. In Chapter 3 we differentiate efficiency from equity, the latter requiring introduction of a social welfare function. The notion of compensation criteria as a means of evaluating alternative economic states is then discussed in Chapter 4. Modifications of the optimizing or Pareto conditions that arise because of market distortions due to imperfect competition, public goods, and externalities are treated in Chapters 5, 6, and 7. Time is then explicitly introduced, and the conditions for dynamic optimization are derived and interpreted.

The next three chapters (9, 10, and 11) analyze the effects of the economy on the distribution of income and policies to alter a given distribution. The formulation of moral or ethical judgments motivating policies of income redistribution are discussed in Chapters 12 and 13 on social choice. Since the ultimate limitation on social welfare is the availability of natural resources, the text concludes with this topic, using the methodology developed earlier.

An effort has been made to maintain consistency of symbols throughout. Subscripts refer to individual consumers or firms while superscripts denote particular amounts of a good or service. References and suggested readings are provided at the end of each chapter.

As is obvious from a reading of the text, my indebtedness to scholars in the area of welfare economics is immense. Students at the College of the Holy Cross have suffered through a number of different versions of the course, which served as the foundation for the text. Special thanks are due to Frank Petrella for his many suggestions on an earlier version, to George Perkins for comments on some of the early chapters, and to Gail Corey for her support and encouragement. Connie Farwell as usual did an excellent typing job with both patience and resignation. I would also like to thank the editors of the *American Economist* for permission to reproduce a part of Chapter 7. Of course, any remaining errors are solely my responsibility.

J.F.O.

CONTENTS

An asterisk (*) indicates a somewhat more mathematical discussion.

WELFARE ECONOMIC THEORY

Chapter 1

THE NATURE OF WELFARE ECONOMICS

Positive economics views the economy as a system susceptible to analysis in ways similar to those used in the natural sciences. It begins with a set of assumptions and derives logical inferences on the basis of these initial premises. For example, having made the assumption that the production function for a firm is "well behaved" and that the firm operates in a purely competitive factor market, we can deduce the cost curves of the firm. The accuracy of such deductions depends crucially on the preciseness of the initial assumptions. Inferences about the slopes of the cost curves depend on the assumptions concerning the substitutability of factors and returns to scale.

Although economists may disagree about the relevance or the realism of a set of assumptions, they generally agree on the economic implications that follow. Economists often question whether the assumptions of perfect competition are appropriate in particular situations, but they tend to agree on what these assumptions imply for the market. Positive economics is concerned with the logical implications derivable from a set of initial assumptions. Disagreements arise over the initial assumptions or because of logical inconsistencies in the derivation of inferences.

Normative economics, quite differently, is concerned with value judgments or ethical statements (sometimes referred to as "ought" propositions) that reflect certain principles or social-ethical norms. Political economy and normative economics may be thought of as synonymous. Normative economics embodies value judgments that are the motivating factor for policy recommendations. For example, those who believe that society suffers from allowing individuals to work at low wages should support a minimum wage. Such a recommendation is based on a value judgment and is made independently of (despite) economic theory, which indicates that such a policy leads to an inefficient allocation of labor.

The relationship between positive and normative statements depends on whether the value judgment is "basic" or would hold under any set of conditions (Sen, 1970). A statement such as, "We ought to have a more equitable distribution of income because it will improve the well-being of society," is normative if it means this result will follow under all circumstances. Purely normative statements cannot be proved or disproved but only accepted or rejected.

Now consider this statement: "We ought to have a more equitable distribution of income because productivity will expand and social welfare will increase." Here we are making a value judgment contingent on some condition being realized (an increase in productivity), and this condition is associated with an improvement in welfare. This recommendation contains elements of both positive and normative economics. Positive economics should enable us to demonstrate the assumptions under which productivity would increase with changes in income distribution and thus imply an increase in welfare.

Welfare Economics

Welfare economics is a varying blend of positive and normative economics. Mishan (1981) uses welfare and normative economics interchangeably and defines them "as the study of criteria for ranking alternative economic situations on the scale of better or worse" (p. 3). In this interpretation welfare economics is much like social choice theory, which is concerned with the development of methods for determining social preferences. In other words, welfare economics develops criteria for assessing economic conditions while social choice theory uses these criteria to evolve rankings. As a simple illustration, welfare economics leads us to conclude that a competitive market system embodies certain desirable attributes, which we will subsequently label *Pareto optimal criteria*. These results are compatible with many different distributions of utility in society, the preferred state is dictated by social choice. Welfare economics is limited to market mechanisms, whereas social choice may be derived through market processes or through political or voting procedures.

Some economists, such as Harberger (1971), would prefer to stress the positive rather than the normative aspects. This position is consistent with the view of economics as a science (a collection of truths), and it would restrict the subject matter of welfare to testable economic hypotheses. Harberger states three postulates of this applied welfare approach:

1. The competitive demand price measures the value of that unit to the consumer.
2. The competitive supply price measures its value to the suppliers.
3. When evaluating costs and benefits of a given action, the costs and benefits accruing to each member of the relevant group should normally be added without regard to the individuals to whom they accrue.

Granted these assumptions, we should be able to formulate testable hypotheses concerning the propriety of various alternatives. In the same way that normative welfare economics overlaps social choice theory, positive welfare is related to public finance and cost-benefit analysis.

The path to be pursued in this text lies somewhere between these limiting cases. First, we want to construct a methodology for determining the goals of society (What does society want, and how much does it want?). We must then decide on the "best" course of action to achieve these objectives, a task that calls for devising certain criteria for determining "best." The particular course of action chosen constitutes a "policy," whose propriety depends on the objective set and the constraints on the economic system.

Constraints

As will be seen, limitations or constraints on the realization of societal objectives will impact in strange and often unexpected ways. These limitations may take on many different forms. Some are technological, determined by the availability of natural resources or the productive structure within the economy. Others are behavioral, determined by hypotheses about individual units in the economy, such as firms maximizing profit or consumers maximizing utility. Obviously, we are constrained by the logical structure in which we operate. Certain conditions will be tautological or contradictory within that structure. These constraints are common to all economic theorizing and, to a degree, to all science. Their effect will differ, however, as the objective differs. The uniqueness of welfare economics is principally with respect to the latter.

An Example: A Commodity Tax

Suppose we have as an objective the redistribution of income to the needy in society. We propose a tax on certain luxury goods, with the intention of allocating the revenue generated to the poor. The positive microeconomic implications of such a policy are that (1) consumption of luxury goods will decline and production of goods for which the poor have a high income elasticity will increase and (2) the utility of the poor should increase while that of the rich (consumers of luxury goods) should decline. Whether such implications represent the "best" policy depends on the collective preferences of society. How important is income redistribution? Is the loss in utility to the rich greater or less than the gain to the poor? Would an income tax or some other program be a better vehicle for realizing the same end? Before addressing these questions, we must comment on the development of welfare economics.

The Evolution of Modern Welfare Economics

Although difficult and often dangerous to generalize, a distinction is sometimes made between neoclassical or "old" welfare economics and new welfare economics. This characterization reflects a change not only in content but also in methodological approach.

Neoclassical ("Old") Welfare Economics

Paul Samuelson (1947) refers to welfare economics prior to 1928 as "ethical hedonism" and includes in this group Pigou, Bentham, Sidgwick, Edgeworth, and Marshall. Despite a multitude of differences, two premises were common to the neoclassical approach. First was the law of diminishing marginal utility, which implied that utility was in some sense quantifiable and that, for any individual, additional units of consumption of a commodity yield smaller (though positive) increases in utility. The second premise was that all individuals had similar utility functions so that the pleasure derived from consumption would be the same for everyone. The pleasure of a concert for one person, for example, would be the same as that obtained by anyone else; more importantly, the value of money (the marginal utility of income) would be the same among all people.

These two assumptions, summarized as utility measurability and interpersonal utility comparisons, had particularly interesting implications when extrapolated beyond the individual to society as a unit. Social welfare could be thought of as the additive sum of the members' utility functions. Assuming the law of diminishing utility and competitive prices, welfare would be maximized when the income of society was uniformly or equally distributed.

"New" Welfare Economics

The "new" welfare economics took form in the discussions associated with repeal of the English Corn Laws in 1846. Harrod (1938) in the neoclassical tradition argued that, though some would benefit and others suffer from repeal, the sum of the gains would exceed the sum of the losses. The decision to repeal thus hinged on the normative judgment that utilities were additive and, therefore, interpersonally comparable.

Kaldor (1939) attempted to separate the economic assessment of the effects of the Corn Laws from any assumptions concerning utility. The Corn Laws should be repealed if those who gain could compensate the losers and still be better off. Kaldor did not suggest that the compensation be actually made—only that it be a possibility. It was the intention of Kaldor and the succeeding "new" welfare economists to separate value judgments from the corpus of economic theory. Efforts to reduce the dependence of policy formulation on the tenets of "utilitarianism" brought about clearer differentiation of the issues of "efficiency" and "equity." Two separate questions were posed: (1) What are the economic implications of a competitive market system with respect to consumption, production, and the relationship between them (efficiency)? (2) Is the resultant distribution of well-being in society consistent with the ethical beliefs of society (equity)?

Efficiency

Vilfredo Pareto (1909) posed a condition for economic efficiency that did not require precise measurability of utility. Efficiency would be achieved when it would not be possible to improve any one person's well-being without adversely affecting that of someone else; there could be no net gains or improvements for anyone in society.

The distinction is often made between *actual* and *potential* Pareto improvements. A change is a potential Pareto improvement if via costless transfers at least one individual could become better off. Such a transfer need never be made, however, for the change to be a Pareto improvement. There are many different versions of the Pareto criterion; for example, we could have substituted the words "everyone" for "anyone," because if at least one person becomes better off, it should be possible via costless transfer to distribute that gain to everyone. A great deal more will be said about this at a later stage. For now it is enough to say that the Pareto criterion as an allocative mechanism to ensure efficiency requires that no potential improvements be possible.

Equity

Under the assumption that Pareto improvements are potential rather than actual, satisfaction of the Pareto criterion is consistent with many (possibly an infinite number) different distributions of income or well-being. Equity addresses the question of the correct or ethical distribution of the product of society. In this context a number of questions will be addressed: What is the distribution given allocative efficiency? Assuming the existing distribution is inappropriate, what devices are available for altering it? What mechanisms are available for determining society's preferences concerning distribution? The first two questions will involve us in the discussion of income distribution and the last that of social choice.

In Chapter 2 we will discuss the competitive market system as a welfare maximizer. In general, it will be relative to the competitive conditions that distortions will be measured and policy recommendations prescribed.

References

Harberger, A. C. 1971. "Three Basic Postulates for Applied Welfare Economics: An Interpretive Essay." *Journal of Economic Literature* 9:785–97.

Harrod, R. F. 1938. "Scope and Method of Economics." *Economic Journal* 48:383–412.

Kaldor, N. 1939. "Welfare Propositions in Economics." *Economic Journal* 49:549–55.

Mishan, C. J. 1981. *Introduction to Normative Economics*. New York: Oxford University Press.

Pareto, V. 1909. *Manuel d'Économie Politique*. Paris: Girard & Brierè.

Samuelson, Paul A. 1947. *Foundations of Economic Analysis*. New York: Atheneum.

Sen, A. K. 1970. *Collective Choice and Social Welfare*. San Francisco: Holden-Day.

Supplementary Readings

Bergson, A. 1938. "A Reformulation of Certain Aspects of Welfare Economics." *Quarterly Journal of Economics* 52:310–24.

Blum, W. J., and H. Kalovern, Jr. 1953. *The Uneasy Case for Progressive Taxation*. Chicago: University Press.

Boulding, K. E. 1969. "Economics as a Moral Science." *American Economic Review* 59:1–12.

Marshall, A. 1920. *Principles of Economics*, 8th ed. London: Macmillan.

Pigou, A. C. 1932. *The Economics of Welfare*, 4th ed. London: Macmillan.

Chapter 2

THE MARKET SYSTEM AS A WELFARE MAXIMIZER

Let us begin with a general discussion of maximizing principles. Assuming maximizing behavior on the part of participants in a competitive market, the long-run equilibrium properties of the system are derived. These characteristics will serve as benchmarks and points of reference in later discussions of market failures.

Maximum Principles

At the very foundation of economics is the assumption, implicit or explicit, that economic units maximize. Their goals or objectives may differ, but a rational economic agent acts efficiently or in a way that maximizes. Paul Samuelson in his acceptance address for the 1970 Nobel Price in Economic Science seems to imply that the very evolution of humankind can be viewed as a maximizing struggle—certainly not deterministic, but rather stochastic and incomplete. The inherent quantitativeness or measurability of many aspects of economics renders easier and more adaptable maximizing techniques. It should be less difficult to test the hypothesis that firms act to maximize profit than the hypothesis that politicians maximize voter goodwill.

Granted that individuals or groups adhere to maximizing principles, two questions that will occupy much of our energy arise: What is the objective or goal being maximized? and What is the appropriate behavior to achieve this objective? The realization of goals will be limited by available resources that enter our analysis as constraints. In this chapter we begin with generally accepted objectives (consumer utility maximization and firm profit maximization) and derive the maximizing conditions.

Because this discussion introduces many concepts from microeconomic theory that will be used throughout the text, our treatment is painstaking and meticulous. Both elementary calculus and geometry, employed as expositional devices, are integrated into the text as a means of reinforcement and in an effort to show their correspondences and analogs. An asterisk (*) precedes the mathematical discussion. The reader might want to avoid the math section on first reading, but for a complete grasp of the relations between methods, the text should finally be read as a unit. A brief review for those whose mathematics is weak is provided in the Appendix.

Duality

Finding extreme values subject to constraints can be viewed in two ways: as maximizing or minimizing problems. One is referred to as the dual of the other. In consumer theory, for example, the household can be thought of as maximizing utility given money income and prices, or as minimizing the cost of achieving a certain utility level. In the first case, the objective is utility maximization, and the constraint is cost. In the second, the objective is cost minimization, subject to a utility constraint. The original problem is called the primal, and the dual is derived from it by interchanging the objective and the constraint. If the primal for the firm is output maximization, subject to a cost constraint, the dual is cost minimization for any output level. As we will see, the operational rules to achieve one objective will simultaneously realize the other. If such is not the case, then our solution to the problem is not feasible. The primal (dual) is sometimes referred to as the flip-flop or mirror image or the dual (primal). A more rigorous demonstration of these results must be deferred to a later section, but knowing these conclusions in advance will enhance our understanding.

Assumptions

Participants

We begin by assuming a perfectly competitive economy in the long run. Later chapters will examine what happens when the assumption is relaxed. Perfect or pure competition implies that no individual consumer or firm is able to exert an appreciable or noticeable effect on either the quantity or price of any good produced or consumed in the market. Individual consumers and firms are "price takers" not "price makers." Participants in the economy have perfect knowledge of the quantities of available commodities and their prices. Products differing in quality are considered different goods. Factors of production are perfectly mobile between uses, and this assumption, coupled with complete knowledge, implies the absence of transaction or exchange cost associated with either consumption or production.

The assumptions of pure competition have often been associated with large numbers of buyers and sellers, each representing an infinitesimal, therefore insignificant, influence on the market. Competition can exist, even in the absence of large numbers, provided the units don't conspire but act independently. Similarly, large numbers don't ensure competition if the economic agents openly or tacitly collude. Each consumer is assumed to maximize his or her utility or satisfaction without being influenced by the behavior of other consumers. Each firm maximizes its profit, again without regard to its effect on other firms or other firms' influence on it.

Commodities

Resources or factors of production are available to any firm in unlimited quantities at the market-determined price (the elasticity of supply of any factor to a particular firm is infinite). The available supply of any commodity to a particular consumer is similarly perceived to be limitless in quantity. Finally, the demand for any firm's output is seen as infinite, as is the demand for any particular unit of a factor of production.

Commodities and factors are assumed to have clearly defined property rights. The contribution of any factor is limited to the firm that employs it, with no spillover or third-person effect. The factor has no other effect than the direct one on output. If coal used to produce steel caused pollution, which decreased the ability of an adjacent laundry to clean clothes, coal would have an indirect effect as well as a direct one. If my listening to music (Bach or the Bee Gees) has an effect on you (favorable or unfavorable), then my consumption is not totally internalized but influences you as well. We will use the phrase *pure private good* to mean that the only effect of a factor or commodity is the direct or immediate one—the one that can clearly be identified as belonging to or being the property of someone.

Time

We will examine the economy at an instant in time after it has fully adjusted to a set of hypothesized conditions. This is referred to as a long-run comparative static analysis. Our examination will focus on the steady state or final equilibrium of the economy without explicitly treating the dynamic required to reach the end result. A comparative static analysis is sometimes metaphorically referred to as a snapshot of the economy at an instant in time. It captures the moment, but says nothing about what led up to this result. Like a snapshot, the long-run conditions for the economy are assumed to remain unaltered and unchanging given the absence of some external influence.

Consumer Theory

An individual's welfare or well-being is assumed to be determined by the goods and services consumed. Noneconomic goods and services have no effect on utility or satisfaction. Preference functions are independent among consumers (i.e., my utility in no way affects yours), so that snob effects, "keeping up with the Joneses," and similar influences are ignored. Consumers are assumed to act rationally or in a way that maximizes their utility or well-being.

Measure of Utility

We could take many different approaches to value the satisfaction or utility derived from consumption. The simplest approach, dating back as far as Jevons (1871) and Walras (1954), hypothesized that satisfaction could be measured in some standard unit. For example, if a steak dinner gave you ten units of satisfaction and a movie five units, we could conclude that the steak gave twice as much satisfaction as the movie. This kind of measurement is called *cardinality*. Although it simplifies things, it doesn't appear to represent the way consumers act, and it begs the question of how one could numerically quantify satisfaction. To base a theory of consumer behavior on the assumption that utility can be measured in the same way one measures apples or pears poses serious conceptual problems.

A far less restrictive assumption, and the one we will use throughout a large part of our discussion, is that of *ordinality*. Ordinal preferences imply that consumers are able to order commodities or commodity bundles in a ranking. For example, one might prefer a steak dinner to a movie, but be unable to affix a number to the preference. Given a choice between the two, the individual would choose a steak dinner. Since we will be assuming a utility function, our solutions will be numeric values. It is important to keep in mind that these numbers simply represent preference rankings and not units of satisfaction.

Before proceeding, it should be mentioned that these methods are not the only ones for evaluating alternatives. Certain parts of our lives are often governed by a "lexicographic" ordering. In such a system we would choose first all those goods with a particularly desirable property before moving on to the next most desired property. All goods with that property would then be chosen in order of the amount of that property possessed. (A dictionary is arranged lexicographically.) It was once believed well-being came from the pursuit of theology and philosophy, and only after one had learned everything possible in these areas should they turn to more menial and debased fields such as economics.

Properties of Individual Preference Orderings

We will restrict our analysis to three commodity bundles, denoted A, B, and C, though generalization to a larger number is straightforward. The consumer is able to rank or order the commodity bundles according to a relation, R, which we will interpret "at least as preferred as."[1] Rationality on the part of the consumer implies the ordering relation satisfies the following three properties:

1. *Completeness:* The preference ranking is complete if for every group of two commodities, either ARB, or BRA, or both (in the latter case the consumer is indifferent [I] between commodity bundles). There is no other possible ordering.
2. *Transitivity:* If ARB and BRC, then ARC. The preference ordering is logically consistent. The condition ARC may imply a strict preference of A over C or indifference (I). A quasi-transitive relation is one such that APB, BPC, then APC.

---

[1] This is frequently referred to as a "weak ordering" since it implies either a strict preference of one alternative over the other, denoted P, or indifference between alternatives, denoted I.

3. *Reflexity:* For each commodity bundle *ARA* (*A* is at least as preferred as itself).[2]

The commodity bundles from which the consumer makes a choice will be determined by his or her money income and commodity prices. The utility-maximizing combination will be that one such that there is no other in his or her choice set for which there is a strict preference (*P*). The bundle chosen will be preferred at least as much as any other bundle in the choice set.

Graphic Exposition

To permit a simple diagrammatic exposition, our discussion will focus on a two-good, two-consumer, two-factor economy. Generalization to the larger dimensions often associated with perfect competition is straightforward. We will denote the utility of a representative consumer by U_i ($i = 1,2$), and it is assumed determined by his or her consumption of two commodities denoted Y_1 and Y_2. Additional units of consumption of each good contribute positively to utility, but at a declining rate. The function is assumed continuous with infinite divisibility of the commodities so we can represent the relation graphically with smooth unbroken curves.

The locus of commodity combinations yielding a particular utility level is called an indifference curve or isosatisfaction curve. A number of such curves are depicted in Figure 2.1*a*,[3] where Y_2 is measured vertically and Y_1 horizontally. Curves farther from the origin represent higher levels of utility indicated by the superscript, and, granted our assumptions, the curves will be negatively sloped, convex to the origin, and nonintersecting.[4] The slope of the indifference curve measures the amount of Y_2 that must be given up as Y_1 is acquired to maintain a

---

[2] You may recall that in terms of sets, a relation (*R*) is reflexive if a set *A* is a subset of itself.

[3] Indifference curves are everywhere dense (i.e. they are really infinite in number, each representing a slightly different utility level).

[4] The heuristic rationale for these assumptions is as follows. Since the utility of each good is positive to maintain total satisfaction, more of one good must be offset by a reduction in the other (negatively sloped). Since incremental utility declines with consumption as we move down an indifference curve, more Y_1 is needed for every unit of Y_2 sacrificed (convexity). If indifference curves intersected, the same commodities would give different levels of satisfaction, which is precluded by assuming a unique correspondence (function) between commodity bundles and utility.

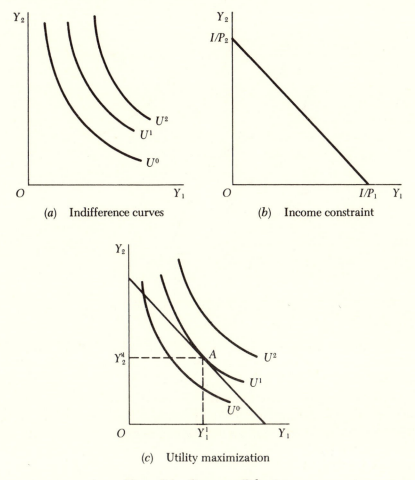

(a) Indifference curves

(b) Income constraint

(c) Utility maximization

Figure 2.1 Consumer Behavior

prescribed utility level. It measures the substitutability of the two commodities in realizing utility. The negative of the slope we will denote as the rate of commodity substitution (RCS).

The goal of the consumer is to reach the highest utility level subject to his or her income (I) and the prices of Y_1 and Y_2, denoted P_1 and P_2, respectively. This constraint can be measured graphically by drawing a straight line with a slope equal to $-P_1/P_2$. The vertical intercept occurs at the maximum quantity of Y_2, purchasable if one's entire income was spent only on it (I/P_2). Similarly, the horizontal intercept is found by dividing income by P_1. The straight line connecting these points is sometimes called the line of "attainable combinations." Any commod-

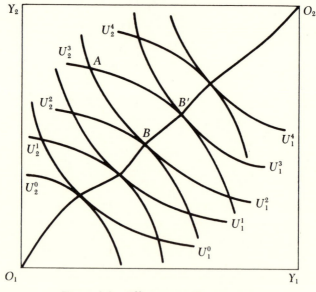

Figure 2.2   Efficiency in Consumption

ity combination along or within the line shown in Figure 2.1*b* is attainable. Since its slope is equal to the (negative) price ratio, it is also called the "price line."

In Figure 2.1*c*, the price line is superimposed on the indifference map. Utility maximization will be realized at the point of tangency between the price line and an indifference curve. At this position, labeled *A* in Figure 2.1*c*, the rate of commodity substitution is equal to the price ratio. No higher utility level can be reached, given money income and prices. Changes in money income with prices constant will be depicted as parallel shifts in the price line, while relative price changes will alter the slope of the price line. From the coordinates of *A* we can determine the level of consumption of each good (Y_1^1 and Y_2^1).

Many Consumers and the Theory of Exchange

Since in a competitive market all individuals face the same prices, utility maximization implies that rates of commodity substitution will be equal among individuals. This need not imply, however, that utility levels are the same, since interpersonal comparisons are ruled out, nor does it imply that the amounts of each commodity consumed will be the same since money incomes will differ.

Equality of rates of commodity substitution ensures Pareto optimality in exchange (i.e., one person's position cannot be improved without lessening that of someone else). A rectangle is constructed in Figure 2.2, the dimensions of which are determined by the available amounts of Y_1 (measured horizontally) and Y_2 (measured vertically). Assuming a two-consumer economy, we will draw the indifference curves of consumer 1 relative to the origin O_1 and those of consumer 2 relative to O_2. The indifference curves are labeled U_i^j, where the subscript denotes the consumer and the superscript the level of utility. The line through the tangency points is called the "contract curve," and it is the locus of Pareto optimal points (i.e., the locus of points where rates of commodity substitution are equal).

Given a position such as A off the contract curve, it is possible through exchange to move to some point in the closed interval BB', where the level of utility of at least one and possibly both increases. The coordinates of any point in the rectangle measured relative to O_1 indicate the amounts of Y_1 and Y_2 consumed by consumer 1, while the coordinates from O_2 indicate consumption by consumer 2. Changes in relative income levels between consumers will generate movements along the contract curve. The process of exchange will ensure attainment of a position on the curve.

*Consumer Behavior

The ordinal utility function characterizing the members of our fictitious economy may be stated formally as:

$$U_1 = U_1(Y_1, Y_2) \quad \text{(utility function of consumer 1)},$$

$$U_2 = U_2(Y_1, Y_2) \quad \text{(utility function of consumer 2)},$$

$$\frac{\partial U_i}{\partial Y_i} > 0 \text{ [marginal utility (MUi) is positive]},$$

$$\frac{\partial^2 U_i}{\partial Y_i^2} < 0 \text{ (marginal utility declining)},$$

$$\frac{\partial^2 U_i}{\partial Y_i Y_j} < 0 \text{ (Y_1 and Y_2 are substitutes)}.$$

The slope of the indifference curves can be derived from the total differential of the utility function (omitting the subscript indicating the consumer):

$$dU = (\partial U/\partial Y_1)dY_1 + (\partial U/\partial Y_2)dY_2. \tag{2.1}$$

Along an indifference curve the change in utility (dU) is zero, so the above can be rewritten as:

$$\frac{-dY_2}{dY_1} = \frac{\partial U/\partial Y_1}{\partial U/\partial Y_2}.$$

The term on the left $(-dY_2/dY_1)$ was defined earlier as the RCS, while the term on the right is the ratio of marginal utilities (MU_1/MU_2). Since the utility of Y_1 declines relative to Y_2 as we move along an indifference curve from left to right, the RCS will decline, and the curve will be convex.

Each consumer has a fixed money income $(I_1$ and $I_2)$ and the prices of Y_1 and Y_2 are fixed at P_1 and P_2. The consumer acts to maximize utility constrained by money income and commodity prices. Using the Lagrange method, the problem may be formulated as follows, where λ represents the Lagrangian multiplier, the subscript i a representative consumer, and the constraint is expressed in implicit form:

$$\max L = U_i(Y_1, Y_2) + \lambda(I_i - P_1Y_1 - P_2Y_2). \tag{2.2}$$

Since our initial assumptions ensure the second-order conditions are satisfied, it is only necessary that the following first-order conditions be met:

$$\frac{\partial L}{\partial Y_1} = \frac{\partial U_i}{\partial Y_1} - \lambda P_1 = 0, \tag{2.3}$$

$$\frac{\partial L}{\partial Y_2} = \frac{\partial U_i}{\partial Y_2} - \lambda P_2 = 0, \tag{2.4}$$

$$\frac{\partial L}{\partial \lambda} = I_i - P_1Y_1 - P_2Y_2 = 0. \tag{2.5}$$

The terms $\partial U_i/\partial Y_1$ and $\partial U_i/\partial Y_2$ are the marginal utilities of Y_1 (MU_1) and Y_2 (MU_2), respectively. For each consumer the ratio of marginal utilities or the rate of commodity substitution (RCS) should equal the ratio of product prices. In addition, each must spend his entire income. As seen from (2.3) and (2.4), the Lagrangian multiplier (λ) is the ratio of the marginal utility to the price for each commodity. It is the marginal utility per dollar spent or the marginal utility of income for consumer i.

The above equations give the necessary conditions to realize our objective (in this case utility maximization). They not themselves tell how much of any good to consume, but they can be solved for these values.[5] Throughout our discussion it will be assumed that the second-order conditions are satisfied.

We mentioned earlier that extremal problems come in pairs. The dual to the above maximizing problem involves minimizing the cost of a particular utility level (U^0). It may be stated as:

$$\min L' = P_1Y_1 + P_2Y_2 + \lambda' [U^0 - U(Y_1, Y_2)]. \qquad (2.6)$$

Applying the same steps as was done previously, it is clear that cost minimization implies equality between the ratio of product prices and the RCS. The Lagrangian multiplier λ' is now the marginal cost or price of an increment in utility, and it is the dual of the marginal utility of income. The Lagrangian is not a real market determined price; rather, it is an inferred or imputed price. For this reason it is often referred to as a "shadow price."

Indirect Utility Functions

In our original formulation of consumer behavior, utility was directly determined by the commodities Y_1 and Y_2 with money income (I) and prices (P_1, P_2) fixed. Income and prices represent the cost of consumer

---

[5] Consider the following simple numeric example, where utility (U) is the product of Y_1 and Y_2; income (I) is 100; the price of $Y_1 (P_1)$ is 5, and Y_2 has a price (P_2) of 10. The maximizing problem will be:

$$L = Y_1Y_2 + \lambda(100 - 5Y_1 - 10Y_2), \qquad (2.2')$$

$$\frac{\partial L}{\partial Y_1} = Y_2 - 5\lambda = 0, \qquad (2.3')$$

$$\frac{\partial L}{\partial Y_2} = Y_1 - 10\lambda = 0, \qquad (2.4')$$

$$\frac{\partial L}{\partial \lambda} = 100 - 5Y_1 - 10Y_2 = 0. \qquad (2.5')$$

From (2.3') λ equals $Y_2/5$, substituting into (2.4') and solving for Y_1 yields $2Y_2$. Finally, substituting for Y_1 in (2.5') and solving Y_2 equals 5 and substituting back in (2.5') Y_1 equals 10. Graphically, these values represent the coordinates of the tangency of the price line and an indifference curve.

satisfaction, and, via the notion of duality, utility maximization implies cost or expenditure minimization. Since utility is not directly measurable, inferences concerning it are often made by examining the expenditure patterns of consumers. These indirect utility functions take the form:

$$C = C(P_1, P_2, U^0);$$

where C is the minimum cost of realizing a utility level U^0 given product prices. Since information on prices and cost is available, indirect utility functions can be estimated empirically and the response of consumers to income and price changes examined.

Production Theory

We will limit our discussion to a firm producing a single product (Y) using two factors of production $(X_1$ and $X_2)$. Each factor is assumed to have a positive but declining effect on productivity. The production function embodies the relationship between factor inputs and the resultant output and assumes technological efficiency. Technology represents the "state-of-the-art" or the various "ways of doing things." A factor input combination is capable of producing many different levels of output, but the maximum level is technologically the most efficient.

Graphic Exposition

Production is represented graphically in two dimensions in Figure 2.3a, with X_2 measured vertically and X_1 horizontally. The curved lines are called "isoquants" and represent the locus of factor input combinations yielding a particular output level. Output will expand as one moves out from the origin. Production functions that are "well-behaved" generate isoquant maps where the isoquants are negatively sloped, nonintersecting, and convex to the origin. The reasoning is analogous to that for the properties of indifference curves, so development of the argument is left to the reader. The slope of an isoquant is a measure of the substitutability of factors. As one moves from left to right giving up X_2 for X_1, the latter (X_1) becomes less easily substitutable for X_2, and the slope declines. The negative of the slope is called the rate of technical substitution (RTS).

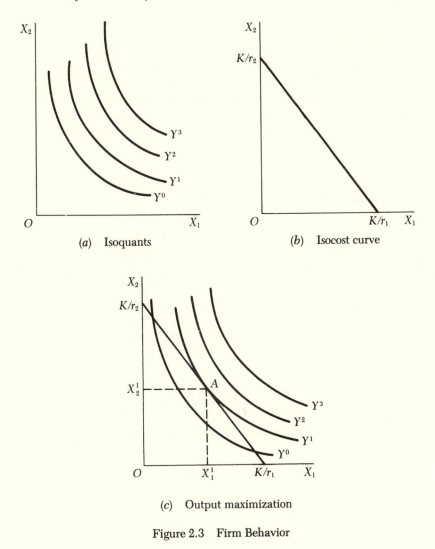

(c)   Output maximization

Figure 2.3   Firm Behavior

The firm attempts to maximize output subject to the prices of X_1 and X_2, denoted r_1 and r_2, respectively, and the funds at its disposal (K). The vertical intercept of this factor price (to be distinguished from our earlier discussion) line is the maximum amount of X_2 attainable (K/r_2), and the horizontal intercept is the maximum amount of X_1 attainable (K/r_1). The slope of the factor price line represented graphically in Figure 2.3b is $-r_1/r_2$. This is often referred to as an *isocost line* because it is the locus of combinations of X_1 and X_2 costing K.

This constraint is superimposed on the isoquant map in Figure 2.3c. The output maximizing position will occur at A, where the rate of technical substitution is equal to the price ratio. The resultant factor combination, consisting of X_1^1 of X_1 and X_2^1 of X_2, will just exhaust the available funds. As the reader can easily verify, changes in the available funds (relative prices constant) are represented by parallel movements of the constraint, while changes in factor prices will alter the line's slope.

*Production Theory

Firms produce a single output, either Y_1 or Y_2. Two substitutable inputs enter the production function in nonnegative amounts X_1 and X_2, and the production function represents the technologically most efficient method of producing any level of output. The marginal physical product (MPPi) of each input is assumed positive but declining:

$$Y_1 = f_1(X_1, X_2) \qquad \text{(production function for } Y_1\text{)},$$

$$Y_2 = f_2(X_1, X_2) \qquad \text{(production function for } Y_2\text{)},$$

$$\frac{\partial Y_i}{\partial X_i} > 0 \qquad \text{[marginal physical productivity (MPP}_i\text{) is positive],}$$

$$\frac{\partial^2 Y_i}{\partial X_i^2} < 0 \qquad \text{(marginal productivity declining),}$$

$$\frac{\partial^2 Y_i}{\partial X_i X_j} < 0 \qquad (X_1 \text{ and } X_2 \text{ are substitutes).}$$

The total differential of the production function is (omitting the subscript for the firm):

$$dY = \partial Y / \partial X_1 \, dX_1 + \partial Y / \partial X_2 \, dX_2. \tag{2.7}$$

Along an isoquant dY equals zero, so rewriting the above yields:

$$\text{RTS} \equiv -dX_2/dX_1 = \partial Y / \partial X_1 / \partial Y / \partial X_2.$$

A representative firm (i) is assumed to have at its disposal funds equal to K_i and to face factor prices of r_1 for X_1 and r_2 for X_2. Its objective is to maximize output given its funds and factor prices, or equivalently to minimize the cost of any level of output.

Again using the Lagrangian technique and deriving the necessary first-order conditions yields:

$$\max L = f_i(X_1, X_2) + \gamma[K_i - r_1X_1 - r_2X_2], \tag{2.8}$$

$$\frac{\partial L}{\partial X_1} = \frac{\partial f_i}{\partial X_1} - \gamma r_1 = 0, \tag{2.9}$$

$$\frac{\partial L}{\partial X_2} = \frac{\partial f_i}{\partial X_2} - \gamma r_2 = 0, \tag{2.10}$$

$$\frac{\partial L}{\partial \gamma} = K_i - r_1X_1 - r_2X_2 = 0. \tag{2.11}$$

The above implies that the ratio of marginal physical products ($\partial f_i/\partial X_1$ and $\partial f_i/\partial X_2$) or the rate of technical substitution (RTS) equals the ratio of factor prices, and that all available funds are spent. The Lagrangian multiplier (γ) is the ratio of the marginal physical product of each input to its price, or the marginal productivity of an additional dollar in funds available to the firm.

The dual of the above would involve minimizing the cost of any particular level of output, say Y^0.

$$\min L' = r_1X_1 + r_2X_2 + \gamma' [Y_i^0 - f_i(X_1, X_2)]. \tag{2.11'}$$

The cost-minimizing conditions are the same as those above with γ being the inputed, or shadow, price of a unit of Y.

Many Firms

The extension of the analysis to many firms is straightforward. Since factor prices will be the same among firms, each will equate the rate of technical substitution to the same price ratio. Firms may have different production functions, produce different goods, and use different quantities of each factor, but the rates of technical substitution will be equal among them.

This can easily be shown graphically using a technique analogous to that used in the discussion of exchange. The dimensions of the rectangle in Figure 2.4a are determined by the available supplies of X_1 and X_2. Assuming only two firms, the isoquants of the first are drawn relative to O_1 and the second relative to O_2. Y_i^j refers to firm i ($i = 1,2$)

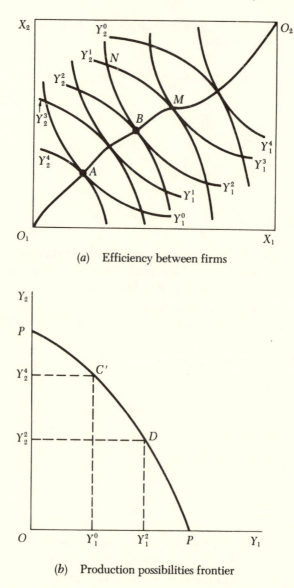

(*a*)   Efficiency between firms

(*b*)   Production possibilities frontier

Figure 2.4   Efficiency in Production

and level of output *j*. From any point off O_1O_2, it is possible to increase the output of at least one, and possibly both, by moving to a position on O_1O_2. Once attained, further increases in the output of one could be achieved only at the expense of the other.

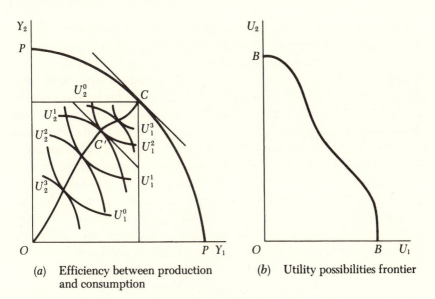

(a) Efficiency between production
     and consumption

(b) Utility possibilities frontier

Figure 2.5   Pareto Optimality

Efficiency Between Production and Exchange

In Figure 2.4b the output combinations ensuring efficiency in production are plotted. Points such as A and B in Figure 2.4a will be mapped into C and D, respectively, in Figure 2.4b. Given our earlier assumptions about the production function, the resultant curve, labeled PP, will be convex to the origin. The negative of the slope $(-dY_2/dY_1)$ is called the rate of product transformation (RPT). It measures how much of one good must be given up for another unit of the other; or the ratio of the marginal cost of Y_1 to that of Y_2. In other words, the RPT is the opportunity cost of producing one good rather than the other; it is the amount of Y_2 (Y_1) foregone when one additional unit of Y_1 (Y_2) is produced assuming efficiency. As shown in Figure 2.5a from any point on the curve, such as C, one can construct a rectangle and the indifference curves of the two consumers, where those for consumer 1 are drawn relative to the origin O and those of consumer 2 relative to C. While every point along the contract curve ensures efficiency in consumption, at one point C' the rate of commodity substitution equals the rate of product transformation; the line drawn tangent to the PP curve is parallel to that drawn tangent to the indifference curves.

Since the RCS is equal to the product price ratio and RPT is equal to the ratio of marginal costs, we can write the above condition as (P_1/P_2) = (MC_1/MC_2). Efficiency between production and consumption ensures that the relative valuation placed on commodities by consumers is just equal to the relative cost of producing them. Corresponding to the points C and C' will be a certain level of utility for each consumer, labeled U_1^2 and U_2^1 in Figure 2.5a. By choosing different points along the product transformation curve, we can derive the utility levels consistent with overall efficiency. The locus of these utility combinations is depicted by BB in Figure 2.5b, where the level of utility of consumer 2 is measured vertically and that of consumer 1, horizontally. This is called the *utility possibilities curve* or *frontier* and represents the various distributions of utility consistent with Pareto optimality. Given our earlier assumptions, we can be reasonably confident the utility possibilities curve will be negatively sloped, but it need not be convex throughout.

The Role of Profits

The term "profits" has many different meanings in economics. It is sometimes used to denote the return to managerial or entrepreneurial services. More often, however, it represents a return to the firm above the total cost of production. It is the likelihood of such a return that motivates firms to undertake production. Profits serve as a link between consumers and producers. The realization of profits requires that firms satisfy consumer needs; therefore, production is channeled into those areas where consumer preferences are greatest.

Since profits are the difference between total revenue and total cost, firms are led to produce those goods for which consumers have the strongest preferences (are willing to pay the highest price) and produce them at the minimum cost. Given our assumptions of perfect competition, the existence of profits will motivate new firms to enter the industry. This process will continue until all the profits are eliminated, which would occur in the long run. Despite the transitory nature of such profits, they are still the driving force of the industrial sector and the nexus between firms and consumers. In the next section we will give a brief mathematical restatement of the Pareto conditions, showing more clearly the role of profits. One final proviso is in order. Although the profit motive in a competitive context ensures the realization of the Pareto conditions, the conditions for efficiency would be the same whether we had a system of private enterprise or some other form of economic organization.

*Efficiency Between Production and Consumption

In the product market the firm is able to sell any level of output produced (Y_i) at a fixed price (P_i). It is assumed the firm will produce that output level that maximizes profit (π_i), defined as:

$$\pi_i = P_i Y_i - r_1 X_1 - r_2 X_2. \tag{2.12}$$

Assuming a production function similar to that used earlier and substituting for Y_i, the first-order maximizing conditions are:

$$\frac{\partial \pi_i}{\partial X_1} = P_i \frac{\partial f_i}{\partial X_1} - r_1 = 0, \tag{2.13}$$

$$\frac{\partial \pi_i}{\partial X_2} = P_i \frac{\partial f_i}{\partial X_2} - r_2 = 0. \tag{2.14}$$

Given that the second-order conditions are fulfilled, profit maximization requires the marginal value product of each factor (MVP), defined as its marginal physical product times product price (MPP·P_i), equal factor price. If the production function is homogeneous of the first degree, Euler's theorem ensures that total factor costs will equal total revenue so that profits will be nonexistent.[6]

---

[6] A homogeneous function is one such that for any $t > 0$,

$$t^n Y = f(tX_1, tX_2),$$

where n is the degree of homogeneity. Euler's theorem ensures that

$$nY = \frac{\partial f}{\partial X_1} X_1 + \frac{\partial f}{\partial X_2} X_2.$$

Letting n equal one and multiplying through by P yields:

$$PY = P\frac{\partial f}{\partial X_1} X_1 + P\frac{\partial f}{\partial X_2} X_2.$$

Profit maximization requires equality of marginal value products and factor prices, so the above may be rewritten:

$$PY = r_1 X_1 + r_2 X_2.$$

Total revenue is just equal to total cost.

From the above, it is obvious that the price of Y_1, P_1 can be expressed as $r_1/(\partial f_1/\partial X_1)$ and P_2 as $r_1/(\partial f_2/\partial X_1)$. Where $r_1/(\partial f_1/\partial X_1)$ is the marginal cost of Y_1 in terms of X_1 and $r_1/(\partial f_2/\partial X_1)$ is the marginal cost of Y_2 in terms of X_1. The ratio of product prices, the rate of commodity substitution, will equal the ratio of marginal costs measured either in terms of X_1 or X_2. Restating,

$$\text{RCS} \equiv P_1/P_2 = \frac{\text{MC}_{1i}}{\text{MC}_{2i}}. \qquad (i = 1,2 \text{ for } X_1 \text{ and } X_2). \qquad (2.15)$$

The ratio of marginal costs is defined as the rate of product transformation (RPT). Efficiency between production and consumption requires that the rate of commodity substitution equal the rate of product transformation.

Pareto optimality is said to exist in a competitive model when consumers and firms act in the above maximizing way and when there is efficiency between production and consumption. The Paretian conditions ensure it is not possible to improve one participant's position without lessening that of another. According to the *Pareto criterion*, any policy that improves the position of at least one person without making anyone else worse off is socially desirable.

Pareto Optimality in a Nonprice Economy

We have just shown that a price system can serve as a vehicle for the realization of Pareto optimality. However, it is possible to think of the Pareto conditions independently of prices, and hopefully, such a view will provide greater insight into the Pareto system.

Consumption

For consumers the Paretian condition requires that each maximize his or her respective utility, given the utility level of the other. We can formalize this as:

$$\max U_1^* = U_1(Y_1, Y_2) + \lambda[U_2^0 - U_2(Y_1, Y_2)], \qquad (2.16)$$

where U_2^0 refers to a prescribed utility level for consumer 2. The first-order maximizing conditions are then:

$$\frac{\partial U_1^*}{\partial Y_1} = \frac{\partial U_1}{\partial Y_1} - \lambda \frac{\partial U_2}{\partial Y_1} = 0, \tag{2.17}$$

$$\frac{\partial U_1^*}{\partial Y_2} = \frac{\partial U_1}{\partial Y_2} - \lambda \frac{\partial U_2}{\partial Y_2} = 0, \tag{2.18}$$

$$\frac{\partial U_1^*}{\partial \lambda} = [U_2^0 - U_2(Y_1, Y_2)] = 0. \tag{2.19}$$

From (2.17) and (2.18) it is obvious that maximization requires equality of the rates of commodity substitution between consumers:

$$\text{RCS}_1 \equiv \frac{\partial U_1/\partial Y_1}{\partial U_1/\partial Y_2} = \text{RCS}_2 \equiv \frac{\partial U_2/\partial Y_1}{\partial U_2/\partial Y_2}.$$

Production

Efficiency in production requires that each firm maximize output, given the output level of the other. The objective function for firm 1, given a level of output Y_2^0 by the firm 2, may be expressed as:

$$\max L_1^* = f_1(X_1, X_2) + \gamma [Y_2^0 - f_2(X_1, X_2)]. \tag{2.20}$$

The relevant first-order conditions are then:

$$\frac{\partial L^*}{\partial X_1} = \frac{\partial f_1}{\partial X_1} - \gamma \frac{\partial f_2}{\partial X_1} = 0, \tag{2.21}$$

$$\frac{\partial L^*}{\partial X_2} = \frac{\partial f_1}{\partial X_2} - \gamma \frac{\partial f_2}{\partial X_2} = 0, \tag{2.22}$$

$$\frac{\partial L}{\partial \gamma} = Y_2^0 - f_2(X_1, X_2) = 0. \tag{2.23}$$

Efficiency requires that the marginal rates of technical substitution be equal between firms.

$$\text{RTS}_1 \equiv \frac{\partial f_1/\partial X_1}{\partial f_1/\partial X_2} = \text{RTS}_2 \equiv \frac{\partial f_2/\partial X_1}{\partial f_2/\partial X_2}.$$

Production and Consumption

Now we must specify the allocation of products and factors between consumers and firms in the economy. Although the determination is straightforward, multiple subscripts that become necessary can be confusing.[7] The point can be simply made by looking at a single consumer who maximizes his or her utility (U), determined by the levels of Y_1 and Y_2 consumed. Y_1 is a function of X_1, and Y_2 a function of X_2, with $\overline{X}_1$ and $\overline{X}_2$ the available supplies of X_1 and X_2. The problem may be stated as:

$$\max L = U(Y_1, Y_2) + \lambda(\overline{X}_1 - X_1) + \gamma(\overline{X}_2 - X_2),$$

$$Y_1 = f_1(X_1),\ Y_2 = f_2(X_2). \tag{2.24}$$

Differentiating with respect to X_1 and X_2 and setting the results equal to zero yields:

$$\frac{\partial L}{\partial X_1} = \mathrm{MU}_1 \mathrm{MPP}_{X_1} - \lambda = 0, \tag{2.25}$$

---

[7] For the hearty soul, the exposition for the more general case is presented. The first subscript of a product or factor will denote the consumer or firm and the second, the product or factor. The value X_{21} is then the input of X_1 to firm 2. Consumer 1 maximizes his or her utility, subject to the prescribed level of consumer 2, denoted U_2^0, the production functions of both firms, and finally the availability of X_1, denoted $\overline{X}_1$, and of X_2, denoted $\overline{X}_2$. Unfortunately, this results in a rather tedious Lagrangian of the form:

$$\max Z = U_1(Y_{11}, Y_{12}) + \lambda_1[U_2(Y_{21}, Y_{22}) - U_2^0] + \lambda_2[f_1(X_{11}, X_{12}) - (Y_{11} + Y_{21})]$$

$$+ \lambda_3[f_2(X_{21}, X_{22}) - (Y_{12} + Y_{22})] + \lambda_4(X_{11} + X_{21} - \overline{X}_1) + \lambda_5(X_{12} + X_{22} - \overline{X}_2).$$

Differentiating with respect to the consumption goods gives the consumption conditions.

$$\frac{\partial Z}{\partial Y_{11}} = \frac{\partial U_1}{\partial Y_{11}} - \lambda_2 = 0, \qquad \frac{\partial Z}{\partial Y_{21}} = \lambda_1 \frac{\partial U_2}{\partial Y_{21}} - \lambda_2 = 0,$$

$$\frac{\partial Z}{\partial Y_{12}} = \frac{\partial U_1}{\partial Y_{12}} - \lambda_3 = 0, \qquad \frac{\partial Z}{\partial Y_{22}} = \lambda_1 \frac{\partial U_2}{\partial Y_{22}} - \lambda_3 = 0.$$

The above implies the rates of commodity substitution will be equal among consumers and equal the ratio of Lagrangian multipliers (λ_2/λ_3).

$$\frac{\partial L}{\partial X_2} = MU_2 MPP_{X_2} - \gamma = 0. \tag{2.26}$$

Rewriting the above yields:

$$\frac{MU_1}{MU_2} = \frac{\lambda/MPP_{X_1}}{\gamma/MPP_{X_2}}. \tag{2.27}$$

Consistent with our earlier discussion, the Lagrangians (λ and γ) represent the effect of marginal changes in resources (X_1 and X_2, respectively) on utility. For this reason they are called the "imputed," "shadow," or "efficiency" prices of X_1 and X_2. Since marginal cost is the factor price divided by the marginal physical product, the right-hand side of (2.27) is the ratio of marginal costs, or the rate of product transformation. It should be clear that any set of factor prices whose ratio equals λ/γ is consistent with efficiency. Market prices are unique only up to a factor of proportionality.

Differentiating with respect to factors yields the efficiency conditions for production:

$$\frac{\partial Z}{\partial X_{11}} = \lambda_2 \frac{\partial f_1}{\partial X_{11}} + \lambda_4 = 0, \qquad \frac{\partial Z}{\partial X_{21}} = \lambda_3 \frac{\partial f_2}{\partial X_{21}} + \lambda_4 = 0,$$

$$\frac{\partial Z}{\partial X_{12}} = \lambda_2 \frac{\partial f_1}{\partial X_{12}} + \lambda_5 = 0, \qquad \frac{\partial Z}{\partial X_{22}} = \lambda_3 \frac{\partial f_2}{\partial X_{22}} + \lambda_5 = 0.$$

The rates of technical substitution will be equal among firms and equal the ratio of Lagrangian multipliers (λ_4/λ_5). Further, each factor will be employed until the ratio of its marginal physical product between alternatives is equal to the rate of commodity substitution (λ_2/λ_3).

Although our analysis has been quite simple, it nevertheless makes the point that Pareto optimality does not require a set of prices for realization. The optimizing rates of commodity substitution equal the ratio of Lagrangian multipliers for the production constraints (λ_2 and λ_3). Similarly, the rates of technical substitution equal the ratio of Lagrangians for the resource or factor constraints (λ_4 and λ_5). We can interpret λ_2 and λ_3 as the "imputed," "shadow," or "efficiency" prices of Y_1 and Y_2, respectively. The imputed prices of the factors X_1 and X_2 are then λ_4 and λ_5. Any set of factor prices such that for any α greater than zero $r_i = \alpha\lambda_i$ (where the subscript of the Lagrangian refers to the factor constraints) will ensure efficiency in production. Any set of product prices such that for any α greater than zero $P_j = \alpha\lambda_j$ (where the subscript of the Lagrangian refers to the production constraints) will ensure efficiency in consumption. In later sections it will be necessary to know to what extent a given set of prices is Pareto efficient.

Pareto Optimality and the Core

The locus of Pareto optimal commodity combinations ensures equality between rates of commodity substitution. No one person's utility can increase without lessening that of someone else. Stated alternatively, a commodity combination Y is Pareto optimal if for any other commodity combination Y',

$$U_i(Y) \geqslant U_i(Y') \qquad \text{for all } i = 1, 2, \ldots, n \text{ and}$$

$$U_i(Y) > U_i(Y') \qquad \text{for at least one } i.$$

In contrast, the "core" is the set of commodity combinations that are not blocked by any coalitions. While Pareto optimality makes no assumptions about the initial distribution of commodities, the core does, and coalitions are formed relative to the initial distribution. With reference to Figure 2.4a, O_1O_2 maps out the locus of Pareto optimal commodity combinations. Assuming an initial distribution at N, those commodity combinations that would not be blocked lie along O_1O_2 between BM. While changes in the initial distribution will change the core, they will not change the set of Pareto optimal points. A point such as A, although on O_1O_2, would be blocked by consumer 1 because his or her utility would be less than at N. The locus of core commodity combinations would never be blocked by any individual or group. Obviously, when the number of participants in the economy increases, the number of possible blocking coalitions rises to infinity. As a consequence, testing whether a particular commodity combination is in the core becomes difficult or impossible. The competitive market system in which all individuals act selfishly in their own interest, given their initial factor endowments or income, leads to an allocation of resources in the core. Since each individual's utility is at least as much as in the initial position, no coalition would block the competitive equilibrium.

Summary

Here we are at the end of a very long but important chapter. Assuming maximizing behavior on the part of consumers and firms, we have derived conditions for economic efficiency that are fundamental to a competitive market system. In the long run the system will move toward the realization of efficiency without any external intervention.

These conditions, however, are not unique to a free enterprise market system; they would also be required for efficient operation of a centrally directed economy.

In this context efficiency implies that there can be no reorganization of the economy in which some participants could improve their positions without adversely affecting others. In a Pareto-efficient economy, gains to one imply losses to another. In a later chapter much of our attention will be focused on trying to measure these trade-offs. One final point should be made. There are many different distributions of utility and, therefore, both commodity and factor combinations consistent with efficiency. Some may involve great inequalities in the distribution of utilities among the members of society. The preferred distribution of utility depends on one's definition of equity. We take the first steps in the examination of equity in the next chapter.

References

Jevons, W. S. 1871. *The Theory of Political Economy*. London.

Walras, L. 1954. *Elements of Pure Economics*, trans. W. Jaffe. London: George Allen & Unwin.

Supplementary Readings

Arrow, K., and T. Scitovsky. 1969. *Readings in Welfare Economics*. London: Allen & Unwin.

Bator, F. 1953. "The Simple Analytics of Welfare Maximization." *American Economic Review* 48:22–59.

Bohm, P. 1973. *Social Efficiency: A Concise Introduction to Welfare Economics*. London: Halsted Press.

Graff, J. De V. 1971. *Theoretical Welfare Economics*. Cambridge: University Press.

Samuelson, P. 1972. "Maximum Principles in Analytical Economics." *American Economic Review* 62:249–61.

Winch, D. M. 1971. *Analytical Welfare Economics*. Harmondsworth: Penguin Books.

Chapter 3

SOCIAL WELFARE MAXIMIZATION

As seen in the last chapter, many different distributions of utility are consistent with economic efficiency or Pareto optimality. We must now devise a method of choosing among efficient points, which in turn requires judgments about the equity of various utility distributions. In this chapter we take the traditional neoclassical approach and assume mechanisms exist for choosing among social states. In our subsequent discussion of social choice the conceptual difficulties associated with such an assumption will be examined.

Community Indifference Curves

In Chapter 2 we derived the locus of utility distributions compatible with a particular output combination (utility possibilities frontier). Alternatively, we could reverse the process somewhat and ask what commodity combinations are consistent with a particular distribution of utilities. A community indifference curve is defined as the locus of these commodity combinations. The indifference curves for consumers 1 and 2 are drawn in Figure 3.1a and b, respectively. We will arbitrarily select the utility levels U_1^2 and U_2^3. At any point on U_1^2, say A, with consumer 1 consuming Y_{11} of Y_1 and Y_{12} of Y_2, where the first subscript refers to the good and the second the consumer, we want to find how much consumer 2 must consume to maintain U_2^3. In addition, to ensure efficiency in consumption, the rates of commodity substitution between consumers must be equal. In Figure 3.1c the indifference curve U_2^3 is superimposed on the indifference map of consumer 1 so that U_1^2 and U_2^3 are tangent at A, requiring the origin of Figure 3.1b to move

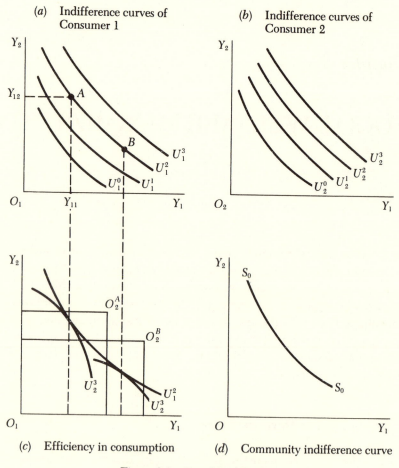

Figure 3.1   Social Preferences

to position O_2^A. The coordinates of O_2^A represent the minimum amounts of Y_1 and Y_2 to realize U_1^2 and U_2^3, which constitutes one point on the community indifference curve.

If we choose some other point such as B remaining along the same indifference curves, O_2^B will constitute another point. Moving along U_1^2 left and right the locus of vertices will map out a community indifference curve labeled $S_0 S_0$ in Figure 3.1d. The slope of $S_0 S_0$ is the marginal social rate of substitution between Y_2 and Y_1. It is the amount of Y_2 that must be given up for a marginal increment in Y_1 to maintain each consumer at a "prescribed" utility level. Given that both goods are consumed by each consumer and the absence of external effects, the marginal social rate of substitution will equal the marginal private rates. Our earlier assumptions about consumer behavior ensure that the curves will be convex for the same reason indifference curves are convex.

One could think now of varying the "prescribed" utility levels and constructing a map or collection of community indifference curves. Since the same commodity combination may be consistent with many different distributions of utility, the curves may intersect. For distributions of utility for which no one is worse off and at least one person is better off, the community indifference curves will be farther from the origin and will be nonintersecting. In such cases one position may be thought of as Pareto superior to another. Community indifference curves allow one to represent social preferences given various utility distributions, but they fail to tell us the best distribution.

Social Welfare Function

The question we must now address is which prescribed utility level is most compatible with social priorities. Using an approach originally developed by Bergson (1938), we will assume a function exists relating distributions of utility to societal welfare (W). Given our two-person society, the form of the function will be:

$$W = W(U_1, U_2). \tag{3.1}$$

It is twice differentiable, and there is a positive association between individual utilities and social welfare.[1] The welfare function embodies ethical convictions of society regarding the importance of individuals 1 and 2. It may be imposed or collectively agreed to, but, at least for now, we'll accept its existence. By holding the level of welfare constant (at say W_0), we can derive the locus of utility combinations relative to which society is indifferent. Three of the infinite number of social welfare contours are depicted in Figure 3.2. Those farther from the origin are unambiguously superior; also, since this collective function embodies individual preferences, we will assume it satisfies the same properties. The social indifference curves are, therefore, negatively sloped, nonintersecting, and convex to the origin.

We concluded our discussion in the last chapter with the utilities possibilities frontier. It represented the locus of utility combinations

---

[1] More precisely we are assuming $\partial W / \partial U_i > 0$, $\partial W / \partial U_i^2 < 0$, $(i = 1, 2)$.

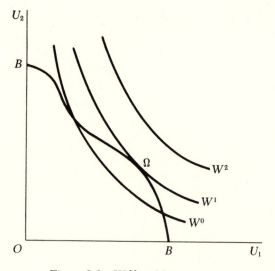

Figure 3.2   Welfare Maximization

attainable, assuming efficiency in production, consumption, and between production and consumption. This schedule is superimposed in
Figure 3.2. The socially optimum position is at Ω, the point of tangency
between BB and W^1. The coordinates of Ω represent the utility levels
of the two consumers. To our previous conditions for *efficiency* we can
now add *equity* in the distribution of society's product.

Most problems in welfare economics are concerned with the joint
issues of efficiency and equity. We want to be sure we are on the utility
possibilities frontier and at that location where welfare is at a
maximum. Equity need not imply *equality*, but rather it refers to some
"just" or "fair," collectively agreed upon method of distributing the
economic fruits of society. In later chapters we will examine the problems involved in deriving such a distributional scheme.

The Role of SWF

In what Samuelson (1947) called the "old welfare economics" of Pareto,
the social welfare function assumed cardinal measurability and interpersonal utility comparisons. Bergson's formulation in terms of an ordinal index was much more plausible theoretically and allowed for a
synthesis between ethical considerations and the conditions for production and exchange. There are those who would argue economists

should concern themselves only with efficiency and abstain from ethical judgments. But even a competitive market system is not devoid of implicit norms and criteria, and even a system achieving total equality implies a set of values. To reward individuals on the basis of their productive contribution and to limit their ability to achieve satisfaction by their income are certainly value statements. It is true that the issues of production and exchange can be addressed using methodologies similar to those in the natural sciences, while these techniques break down in the treatment of equity, but one must not confuse technique with content. Samuelson sums up the relationship between the issues of efficiency and equity as analogous to "saying it does not matter whether or not a man has hair so long as it's curly!"

A Look Backward

Despite the adage "not to look backward because someone might be gaining on you," it will help to summarize our discussion thus far if we consider what can be inferred from the maximizing position Ω in Figure 3.2.

1. Knowing Ω we can find the utility levels of consumers.
2. Combinations of commodities yielding these levels can then be determined.
3. Given the production functions and output levels, the factor input combinations can be derived.
4. Assuming efficiency, rates of commodity and factor substitutions can be determined, and from these product and factor prices up to a factor of proportionality.

We could introduce money as a *numeraire* permitting the derivation of absolute prices, but that would take us too far afield. Although for convenience we have limited our discussion to the two-dimensional case, it could easily be extended. Until now we have assumed perfect competition, but in later chapters we will begin to discuss what happens when we have market distortions.

References

Bergson, A. 1938. "A Reformulation of Certain Aspects of Welfare Economics." *Quarterly Journal of Economics* 3:310–34.

Samuelson, P. A. 1965. *Foundations of Economic Analysis.* New York: Atheneum.

Supplementary Readings

Mishan E. J. 1981. *Introduction to Normative Economics*. New York: Oxford University Press.

Scitovsky, T. 1942. "A Note on Welfare Propositions in Economics." *Review of Economic Studies* 9:77–88.

Chapter 4

SURPLUS AND COMPENSATION

Since one never knows how close the economy is either to Pareto optimality or social welfare maximization, some policy prescriptions must be considered. One could argue that barring intervention, the competitive system will tend inexorably toward general equilibrium. Yet policies still need to be judged with reference to the speed with which they facilitate such movement, and, in the absence of competition, criteria must be devised for assessing market states relative to competitive conditions. This chapter continues the assumptions of a competitive market, while in the next chapter the assumptions are relaxed. The notion of comparability of alternative economic states is fundamental to any discussion of economic policy. We have all read about cost-of-living increases that reduce real income and, as frequently inferred, reduce social welfare. But what are the measures used to arrive at this conclusion, and what is the base from which changes are gauged? Do alternative measures lead us to the same conclusion quantitatively or qualitatively? These issues are now discussed and applied to the problem of index numbers and cost-benefit analysis.

Surplus

Evaluation of economic policies involves some relative assessment of the benefits to those who gain and the losses to those who suffer. Generically, a surplus is a return or benefit above economic or opportunity cost. "Consumers surplus" arises when the utility or satisfaction derived from consumption of a good exceeds the price of the good. In a competitive economy with a downward-sloping demand schedule, consumers pay for all commodities the value of the last unit to them. The value of units consumed prior to the last unit exceeds the price, thus generating a surplus.

Analogously, given an upward-sloping supply schedule, the firm charges for all units of a good produced the cost of the last unit. All previous units cost less to produce than the price at which they are sold. This difference between costs and price is called "producers surplus." Finally, "factors surplus" or "rent" arises when the return to a factor is in excess of its contribution to production. The issue involved in the notion of surplus is not one of existence but of measurability. Our discussion will focus on consumers surplus, since for our purposes it is the most important, but many of our remarks have more general applicability.[1] We will begin by looking at an individual consumer and then discuss the problems of measurability among consumers.

Measurability of the Surplus

Consider an individual with income I^1 who purchases commodities Y_1^1 of Y_1 and Y_2^1 of Y_2 at prices P_1^1 and P_2^1. Letting $\overline{Y}^1$ denote the commodity vector of set Y_1^1 and Y_2^1, consumer utility can be represented as $U(\overline{Y}^1)$. The price of Y_1 decreases to P_1^2, with all other prices and money income held constant. There will now be a new set of commodities Y_1^2 and Y_2^2 and a new level of utility $U(\overline{Y}^2)$. The following are possible ways of measuring the change in the surplus generated by the price change:

1. The change in utility: $U(\overline{Y}^2) - U(\overline{Y}^1)$;
2. The area under the demand curve of Y_1 between the prices P_1^1 and P_1^2;[2]
3. The amount of income that must be taken away given the new prices so that the utility (income) of the individual is the same as it was originally (compensating variation);
4. The amount of income that must be given to the individual at the original prices so that his utility (income) is the same as it is after the price change (equivalent variation).[3]

Alfred Marshall (1920) who is principally responsible for developing

---

[1] The grammarian may wonder why an apostrophe was not used to show the possessive case when defining the various kinds of surplus. The notion of surplus has been applied at both the individual and aggregate levels often without differentiation. When considering measurability, however, aggregation adds additional problems. The issue of measurability is two-pronged: (1) whether for a particular unit (consumer, firm, or factor) it is possible to measure the surplus (apostrophe before the "s") and (2) whether one can aggregate the surplus over units (apostrophe after the "s").

the notion of surplus implies that all these measures are equivalent. Hicks (1956), Samuelson (1950), and others have demonstrated that in general this is not the case. We will discuss each measure in turn trying to show its similarities and differences with the others.

Precise quantification of measure 1 requires that utility be precisely measurable or measurable in cardinal terms. If it is not, the difference in utility levels can only be interpreted as an ordering of preference states. Under some circumstances, it may be sufficient to know simply that one state is better than another, but more often one would want some measure of the difference. In addition, for policy purposes it is necessary to have a measure of the total or collective surplus. This, in turn, requires that utility be comparable between individuals (i.e., that we be able to add the utilities of different people). Measure 2 rectifies some of these problems by allowing utility to be measured in terms of a common denominator or *numeraire*.

Measure 2 expresses the effect of the price change on utility in dollars terms; however, for such a measure to be accurate, the *numeraire* must be an invariant. More precisely, the marginal utility per dollar must be the same at P_1^1 and P_1^2. Since price changes imply changes in real income, we must assume the marginal utility of income is a constant. Critics have argued that it is unreasonable to believe an

---

[2] Letting $d(Y_1)$ represent the consumer's demand schedule for Y_1, the measure would be the shaded area in Figure 4.1. Defined mathematically, it would equal:

$$-\int_{P_1^1}^{P_1^2} d(Y_1) dP_1.$$

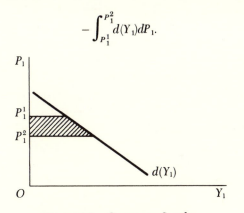

Figure 4.1   Consumer Surplus

[3] In both measures 3 and 4, the income change will not, in general, be invariant with respect to the level of utility at which the consumer is held. As Silberberg (1972) and others have shown, this will be the case only when indifference curves are vertically parallel.

additional dollar yields the same utility when one's income is $5,000 as it does when it's $50,000. Marshall would respond by saying his analysis has reference to very small (infinitesimal) changes in real income where constancy of the marginal utility of income is an acceptable assumption. The problem of making comparisons between individuals with varying incomes, however, still remains. J. R. Hicks in a book entitled *A Revision of Demand Theory* (1956) breathed new life into the notion of consumers surplus by showing that it could be quantified independently of the assumption of cardinal measurability or constancy of the marginal utility of income.

Compensating Variation (Surplus)

Measures 3 and 4 can best be illustrated by referring to Figure 4.2, with money income measured vertically and Y_1 consumed measured horizontally.[4] Initially the consumer is at the utility-maximizing position A, with income denoted by I^1I^1 and utility by U^1. The price of Y_1 declines to P_1^2, represented by the slope of I^1I^2, and a new equilibrium is reached at B at utility level U^2. We can now ask by how much must income be decreased, given the new price, to move the consumer back to U^1 from U^2. The answer can be found by drawing a line (I^3I^3) parallel to I^1I^2 but tangent to U^1. The compensating variation in income is equal to the differences between the income I^1 and I^3 $(I^1 - I^3)$. Note that the tangency point is C, indicating that the amount of Y_1 (and therefore Y_2) consumed is different than it is at either A or B. The "compensating variation" assumes the consumer will adjust his consumption of all commodities given a price change for one of them. It is the minimum income change necessary to maintain the original utility level, and at position B it is represented by the line segment BG.

We could take a slightly different approach and ask, given the price change and the new utility-maximizing level of Y_1, by how much must income be reduced to maintain at the original utility level. Unlike the previous situation, the amount of Y_1 consumed is not allowed to change. This is denoted by the line segment BF in Figure 4.2, and it is called the "compensating surplus."

---

[4] Y_2 could have been measured vertically instead of income and our discussion conducted in terms of relative prices. Changes in the price of Y_1 imply relative price changes. Similarly, changes in income, unless contrary assumptions are made, will lead to increases in both Y_1 and Y_2 consumed. All the assumptions of earlier chapters concerning consumer behavior are relevant.

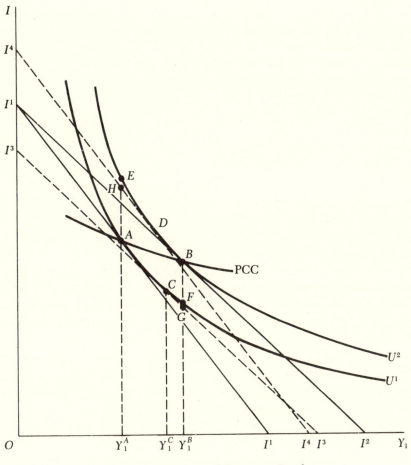

Figure 4.2   Measures of Consumer Surplus

Equivalent Variation (Surplus)

Using the same figure, we could ask by how much income would have to increase given the original price to be just as well off as at the new price. By how much must income increase with the price of Y_1 equal to P_1^1 to permit a level of utility U^2? Obviously, the answer can be found by drawing a line parallel to I^1I^1 but tangent to U^2. Denoting this line by I^4I^4, the "equivalent variation" in income will be the difference between the income level I^4 and I^1 (AH). The tangency point is D, indicating that although the utility level is the same as at B, the utility-maximizing commodity bundle is not.

The equivalent variation is the minimum increase in income to achieve U_2. If the consumer maintains a constant level of Y_1, then income would have to be increased an amount equal to AE to realize the new utility level. The increase in income required, assuming initial prices and the initial level of Y_1 consumed, is called the "equivalent surplus."

Relations Between Measures

As an exercise you should assume an increase in price rather than a decrease. You will find that the equivalent (compensating) variation for a price fall (rise) is equal to the compensating (equivalent) variation for a price rise (fall). The same holds for compensating and equivalent surpluses.

The change in the quantity of Y_1 demanded can be divided into an income and a substitution effect, and for relatively small price changes the former can be ignored. Making this assumption with reference to Figure 4.2 means points A and D must be on a straight line perpendicular to the horizontal axis since (1) the slopes of the price lines are equal at A and D, (2) there is no substitution effect, and (3) the difference in income can be ignored. Exactly the same conditions hold for points B and C. In the absence of an income effect, all measures of variation or surplus would be equal.

Marshall (1920) assumed the marginal utility of income was a constant because the income change was so small. This may be interpreted in the Hicksian analysis as a zero income effect. It must be kept in mind, however, that a zero income effect and a constant marginal utility of money are not equivalent assumptions.

An Alternative Approach—Compensated Demand Schedules

Many would argue that the contribution of economists is not what they say but the many ways they have of saying it. In this section, we look at an alternative way of analyzing the notions of compensating and equivalent variation. To avoid some rather tedious geometry, derivation of the corresponding surpluses is restricted to footnotes. For a more complete discussion of the latter, the interested reader is referred to D. M. Winch (1971).

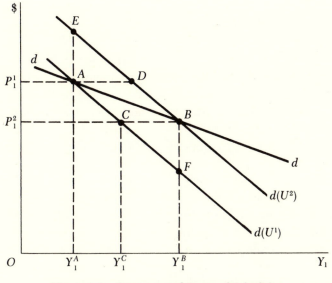

Figure 4.3   Compensated Demand Schedules

The locus of utility-maximizing positions, given changes in relative prices with money income constant, is called a price consumption curve and is denoted PCC in Figure 4.2. From each point on the curve we can find the quantity of Y_1 demanded at a particular price. The locus of these price and quantity combinations constitutes the demand schedule for Y_1 by a particular consumer. It is denoted dd in Figure 4.3, where the points A and B correspond to the same points as in Figure 4.2. The *compensated demand* curve measures the quantity demanded at various prices assuming money income is adjusted so that the level of utility is the same at every price and quantity. The curve $d(U^1)$ assumes utility is held constant at U^1. The points A, C, and F in Figure 4.2 will all lie on $d(U^1)$. The curve $d(U^2)$ represents the compensated demand schedule for utility equal to U^2 with points E, D and B.

By construction the income effect is zero along a compensated demand curve. Increases (decreases) in income permitting increases (decreases) in utility will shift the curve out (back). The compensating variation assumes utility is maintained at U^1 and equals the area under the compensated demand $d(U^1)$ between prices P_1^1 and P_1^2 or $P_1^1ACP_1^2$. This area is equal to $I^1 - I^3$ in Figure 4.2. The equivalent variation assumes a utility level U^2 and is measured as the area under the compensated demand curve $d(U^2)$ between P_1^1 and P_1^2 or $P_1^1DBP_1^2$. The latter is equal to $I^4 - I^1$ in Figure 4.2.[5]

Measure 2 defined the consumers surplus as $P_1^1ABP_1^2$. If there were no income effect, this ordinary demand schedule would be the same as the compensated demand schedule, and measures 2 thru 4 would correspond. Marshall (1920) defined consumers surplus as the difference between what a consumer would have to pay for each unit of a commodity if it were provided by a perfect price discriminator and what is actually paid in a competitive market. In the former case each unit would be sold at the maximum amount the consumer would be willing to pay. Obviously, such hypothetical situations do not arise in reality, and the issue centers on how this difference can be ascertained. Thus far our discussion has concerned a single consumer, but for many policy issues some measure of the aggregative or collective surplus may be necessary. As alluded to earlier, whether an aggregate consumers surplus is meaningful depends on whether a common measuring rod or *numeraire* for income or surplus changes among individuals can be found. It is to the issue of interpersonal comparisons that we now turn.

Compensation Criteria

A Pareto optimum occurs when it is no longer possible to improve one individual's position (utility) without adversely affecting that of some other. Most economic policies, however, involve redistributions; some individuals gain while others suffer. The issue then becomes whether the benefits of those who gain are greater than the losses to those who are harmed. If the answer to this rhetorical question is in the affirmative, such a change would lead to a hypothetical improvement in social welfare.

To clarify subsequent discussion, we will begin by defining the com-

---

[5] The compensating surplus assumes Y_1 consumed remains at B rather than moving to C. Therefore, the decrease in income (BF in Figure 4.2) will be less than for the compensating variation (BG). At a price P_1^2, if Y_1^B rather than Y_1^C units were consumed, additional income of $Y_1^CCBY_1^B$ in Figure 4.3 would be needed. The additional surplus would be $Y_1^CCFY_1^B$ and the difference CBF. This corresponds to FG in Figure 4.2. It measures the additional compensation required because a level of Y_1^B is not maintained. The compensating surplus will equal the compensating variation ($P_1^1ACP_1^2$) minus the amount (CBF) in Figure 4.3, or BG minus GF in Figure 4.2. You should be able to explain why the equivalent variation is equal to $P_1^1DBP_1^2$ in Figure 4.3 and the equivalent surplus $P_1^1DBP_1^2$ plus AED. This corresponds to AH plus HE in Figure 4.2.

pensation criteria devised by N. Kaldor (1939), J. R. Hicks (1940), and T. Scitovsky (1941).

> *Kaldor criterion:* Given two alternatives A and C, C is socially preferred to A if those who gain can compensate those who lose and still be in a better position (have a greater level of utility).
> *Hicks criterion* (the "reverse" test): C is socially preferred to A if those who lose cannot profitably bribe those who gain into not making the change.
> *Scitovsky criterion* (the "double" test): C is socially preferred to A if those who gain can bribe those who lose into accepting the change and, simultaneously, those who lose cannot bribe those who gain into not making the change.

Scitovsky showed that it may be possible to satisfy either the Kaldor or Hicks criterion but not both. It is important to keep in mind that none of these tests requires that compensation actually be paid, only that it could be made.

BB in Figure 4.4 represents the locus of utility possibilities in a

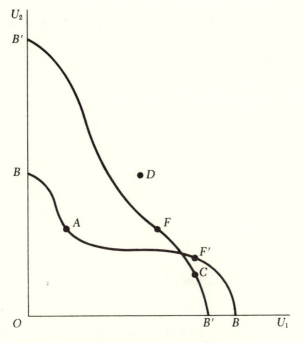

Figure 4.4   Compensation Criteria

two-person economy prior to a policy change, and $B'B'$ represents the locus after the change. The derivation of these curves was discussed in Chapter 2. All points along the curves are consistent with Pareto optimality.

Consider a policy change that involves a movement from A to C. This would be socially preferred given the Kaldor criterion because the winners (U_1) could compensate the losers (U_2) and still be better off. At F_3, U_2 is the same as at A, but U_1 is greater than at A. Using the Hicks criterion, one cannot say this change is socially preferred. The losers (U_2) could bribe the winners (U_1) into not making the change. At F', U_1 remains unchanged, but the decrease in U_2 is less than at C. The bribe would be less costly than the policy change to C.

Consider a movement from C to D, in which the Hicks criterion would lead to acceptance: the losers (U_1) could not bribe the winners (U_2) into not choosing D. (There is no point on $B'B'$ where U_2 is greater than at C and U_1 is no less than at C.) The Kaldor test could not be applied since the utility loci at D (after the change) are unknown.

In some discussions (e.g., Winch, 1971, among others), the Kaldor and Hicks criteria are combined into the Kaldor-Hicks compensation test. Both criteria involve hypothetical compensations and, therefore, potential welfare changes. Scitovsky showed that if the utility loci before and after the change intersect, a contradiction may occur in applying the two tests. He argued a true improvement in welfare would occur in moving from A to C if the utility locus through C passes outside of A and that through A passes inside of C. Samuelson (1950) has shown, however, that the "double" test of Scitovsky does not preclude intersections entirely, but rather excludes an odd number of intersections between A and C. It does not preclude an even number of intersections outside A and C.

Since none of the measures we have discussed requires actual income redistributions, transaction costs involved in such hypothetical changes are ignored. In addition, nothing is implied with respect to the initial distribution of welfare. The discussion is entirely in relative terms.

Little Criterion and Samuelson Criterion

I. M. D. Little (1949) shows the interdependencies between considerations of relative efficiency (implicit in the above tests) and of distributional equity (implicit in the formulation of social welfare functions). He proposes two measures: (1) that the new utility (income) distribution be no worse than the old and (2) that it not be possible to make everyone as well off in the original position as after the change. The latter is effectively the Scitovsky criterion, while the former implies a social welfare function along the lines of Arrow, Bergson, and Samuelson. Little emphasizes the importance of being able to measure the social welfare implications of alternative utility (income) distributions both before and after a change in policy.

Samuelson proposes that for every possible distribution of utility, both before and after the change, the Scitovsky test must be satisfied. With reference to Figure 3.5 in the previous chapter, a change is socially preferred if the point of tangency between the utility possibility locus and the social welfare contour after the change is at a higher level of social welfare, and the utility possibilities curve after the change lies everywhere outside that prior to the change. The distribution of utilities after the change is thus socially preferred, and no possible redistribution could improve social welfare.

Undoubtedly, the above discussion appears quite abstract and obtuse, yet the concepts involved have many real-world analogs. We will apply these ideas to the problem of index numbers and cost-benefit analysis.

Index Numbers

In practice we do not have utility loci before and after a change; rather, we have some current and some previous or base value of an economic variable. On the basis of this information we want to make a relative comparison. To correct for spurious inferences due to price changes, national income accounts are adjusted using price indices. The formulas for Laspeyre's index (L) and Paasche's index (P) are as follows:

$$L = \frac{\Sigma P_{in} Y_{i0}}{\Sigma P_{i0} Y_{i0}} \cdot 100,$$

$$P = \frac{\Sigma P_{in} Y_{in}}{\Sigma P_{i0} Y_{in}} \cdot 100,$$

where P_{in} and Y_{in} refer to the price and quantity of good i purchased in time period n; P_{i0} and Y_{i0} refer to the price and quantity of i in period 0; and the summation extends over a representative set of commodities.

By dividing money income in period n ($\Sigma P_{in} Y_{in}$) by Laspeyre's index (in decimal form), one can determine income in period n measured at period 0 prices and assuming the distribution of Y at period 0. Laspeyre's index asks whether, given the distributional weights of the original situation, the new position is better. This is in effect the Hicks criterion since we are considering the initial distribution of income (A). Paasche's index asks whether, given the new distribution of Y in n and valued at period 0 prices, income is greater or less. If the distribution of Y were as it is in the new situation, would income be greater before or after the change? This is analogous to the Kaldor criterion.

It should be obvious that in our original discussion we were concerned with distributions of utility and the effect on social welfare. Index numbers refer to distributions of commodity purchases and their effect on national income. The issue of the appropriate frame of reference and benchmark of comparison are the same, however. Generally, national income data are deflated by a single price index so that one but not both criteria are applied. Many economists have suggested the need for double deflating to determine income changes more accurately and unequivocally.

Cost-Benefit Analysis (C-B)

Cost-benefit analysis is an attempt to implement empirically the above notions of surplus and compensation. The basic criterion of C-B is to maximize benefits in relation to costs given some policy change. The former are interpreted as those effects that increase the value of the objective function (welfare) while the costs reduce it. Since it is not possible to measure all the consequences of an action, C-B is generally limited to first-order influences, and, as such, it is a partial equilibrium analysis. The two most difficult problems associated with C-B are the specification of the objective function and the measurement of the effects of a change.

The following example may help to illustrate some of the issues involved. Decision makers in a relatively less developed country contemplate the introduction of new methods of agricultural production. Since the necessary technology must be imported, these direct costs are known. Production is a function of land and labor, and it is further assumed that the arable land is fixed in size and that agriculture is competitive. The total product of labor schedule before the change is depicted by TP_0 in Figure 4.5a. From the total product schedule, the demand schedule for labor (D_L^0) can be derived. Given a labor supply schedule S_L in 4.5b, the level of employment will be L_0 at a wage W_0, from the production function L_0 will generate an output level Q_0.

Depicting the product market by D in 4.5c, Q_0 will be sold at a price P_0. The improved technology shifts the total product schedule to TP_1, and by increasing labor's productivity, shifts the factor demand to D_L^1. The new level of output Q_1 will sell at a price P_1.

The benefit of this change is the value of the additional agricultural production, measured by Q_0ABQ_1. The cost is the direct cost of the change plus the opportunity cost of the additional labor employed, represented by L_0EFL_1. Clearly, the precise measurement of costs and benefits requires knowledge of both the product demand and factor supply schedules.

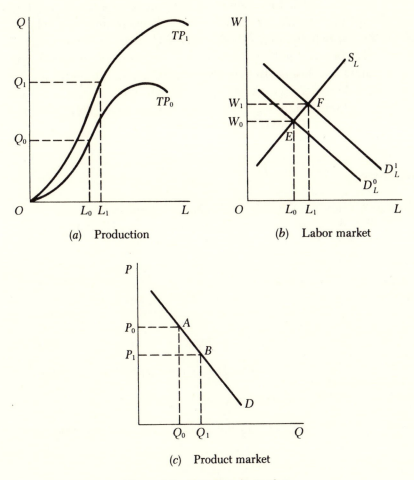

(a)   Production   (b)   Labor market

(c)   Product market

Figure 4.5   Cost-Benefit Analysis

In many cases our concern may be as much with the distributional effects of a policy as with the overall costs and gains. In the above example, the gain to consumers is the consumer surplus, which we will assume is measurable by $P_1 P_0 AB$ in 4.5c, while the gain to the workers or factor surplus is represented by $W_0 W_1 EF$ in 4.5b. Finally, the difference between total revenue and total cost before and after constitutes the change in the rental value of land $(OP_1 BQ_1 - OW_1 FL_1) - (OP_0 AQ_0 - OW_0 EL_0)$. Costs and benefits can be measured in terms of changes in surplus, but the latter are the same gains and losses looked at in distributional terms. Adding a measure of surplus to the value of inputs or outputs would entail double counting. In other words, the value of the additional wheat produced redounds to the benefit of consumers and the factors used in production. The notion of surplus is an attempt to measure the distributional effects of the policy change. Even though benefits may exceed costs, a change may be undesirable from a distributional perspective. Policy evaluations require identifying the winners and losers. In practice, even the measurement of direct costs and benefits, let alone distributional effects, may be quite difficult. Yet understanding the underlying theory will often prevent us from drawing overly simplistic conclusions.

References

Hicks, J. R. 1940. "The Valuation of Social Income." *Economica* 7:105–24.
———. 1956. *A Revision of Demand Theory*. London: Oxford University Press.
Kaldor, N. 1939. "Welfare Propositions and Interpersonal Comparisons of Utility." *Economic Journal* 49:549–52.
Little, I. M. D. 1949. "The Foundations of Welfare Economics." *Oxford Economic Papers*, New Series 1:235–37.
Marshall, A. 1920. *Principles of Economics*, 9th ed. London: Macmillan.
Samuelson, P. A. 1950. "Evaluation of Real National Income." *Oxford Economic Papers*, New Series 2:18–21.
Scitovsky, T. 1941. "A Note on Welfare Propositions in Economics." *Review of Economic Studies* 9:77–88.
Silberberg, E. 1972. "Duality and the Many Consumer's Surpluses." *American Economic Review* 42:942–52.
Willig, R. D. 1976. "Consumer's Surplus Without Apology." *American Economic Review* 66:589–97.
Winch, D. M. 1971. *Analytical Welfare Economics*. Harmondsworth: Penguin.

Chapter 5

REGULATION IN IMPERFECTLY COMPETITIVE MARKETS

In some sectors of the economy, satisfying the Pareto conditions may be impossible, while in others attainment of the marginal conditions may be inconsistent with welfare maximization. In this chapter we consider the effects of monopolistic practices on the realization of optimality. We begin by discussing the distortions arising because of market imperfections, and then we address policies aimed at the distorted sector. In the final section we consider policies appropriate in other parts of the economy when the market imperfections in a given sector cannot be eliminated.

A monopolist is able to exercise discretionary power over either the price or the aggregate quantity of a good or service produced (i.e., the demand schedule for the firm is downward sloping). In addition, the monopolist is able to earn an above-normal return, which is referred to by A. P. Lerner (1933–34) as *monopoly revenue* and is equal to total revenue minus total cost. This return is in excess of the firm's full cost of production, including a normal return to the entrepreneur. Unlike the competitive firm, this return can persist even in the long run because of barriers precluding entry into the industry. Sometimes the nature of the product may not lend itself to many firms, in which case the barriers are referred to as *natural*. This is particularly likely to be the case with goods or services requiring physical connections. In a given locality, for example, having several sewerage disposal companies, or electric power companies, or even independent telephone companies would not be efficient. Further, in most cases, production requires very large initial capital investments, the cost of which is prohibitive to many potential competitors. Possibly the nature of the market rather than of the firm precludes multiple providers. A local area may be able to support a single airport with a profit, but if there were two airports, neither one could meet total cost.

Often the term *monopoly* is used to denote the more pernicious case in which the barriers to entry are *artificial*—that is, they arise from deliberate obstructionist behavior by the monopolist, who may, for example, buy up the sources of supply or the raw materials needed in production, thus precluding others from producing. This situation, referred to as vertical integration, implies that the monopolist, or one of the subsidiaries, would own the resources at every stage in the production process. For example, the automobile producer would own the steel mill, the tire producer, and so on.

The monopolist may also obstruct competition by adopting a pricing policy that hinders entry. Rather than setting price at the profit-maximizing level, the monopolist may set one high enough to ensure a profit but not high enough to provide an incentive to potential competitors. Legislation may also serve to artificially limit competition. Tariff and import restrictions lessen competition from abroad, which reduces rivalry in areas such as shoes, automobiles, and so forth. License requirements, although their intention might be to ensure quality, lessen competition among electricians, plumbers, and even physicians.

Maximizing Behavior

In the competitive model, profit maximization implied equality of price (P) and marginal cost (MC), since profit (π) equaled total revenue (TR) minus total cost (TC), and each firm was a price taker. For the monopolist, price is not a constant, so that the first-order maximizing condition is now not price but marginal revenue equals marginal cost.[1] For the monopolist, marginal revenue will be less than price for all

---

[1] Profit will be defined as

$$\pi = PY - CY,$$

where P is the price of Y and C average cost. The first-order maximizing condition is then

$$\frac{\partial \pi}{\partial Y} = \frac{\partial P}{\partial Y}Y + P - \left(\frac{\partial C}{\partial Y}Y + C\right) = 0.$$

units greater than the first. Since all units sell at a single price as we move down the demand schedule, we must subtract from total revenue the loss in revenue from earlier, higher-priced units.

Monopoly Distortion

Figure 5.1 attempts to approximate the distortive effects of monopoly. We will assume a long-run context with average cost increasing because of diseconomies of scale. It could also be due to monopsonistic factor market conditions; however, consideration of these will be deferred until our discussion of income distribution. In the former case factors become relatively less productive as output expands. In the latter, the return to factors must be increased as more are hired.

The competitive price and quantity are denoted P' and Y', respectively, and the monopolist values P and Y. The loss in consumers surplus attributable to monopoly is $PABP'$. The loss in factor return is $CDBP'$. Monopoly revenue is $PADC$. As can be seen, the monopoly revenue is in part extracted from the consumers surplus $P'PAE$ and in part from factor rent $CP'ED$. The net social loss is equal to the loss in consumers surplus plus the loss in factor rent minus the monopoly revenue or ABD in Figure 5.1. This loss is referred to by Harberger (1974) and others as "dead-weight" loss.[2]

Alternative Measurement

Although appealing, Lerner (1933–34) points out that the above analysis is limited because the measures derived depend for their values on the shapes of the cost and revenue curves between Y and Y'. The competitive price (P') and quantity (Y') are not realized (indeed, they

---

Denoting the term in parentheses as marginal cost MC and multiplying and dividing the marginal revenue $[(\partial P/\partial Y)Y + P]$ by P gives $P(1 + 1/\eta) = $ MC, where η is the elasticity of demand for Y. The second-order condition requires that $\partial^2 \pi/\partial Y^2 < 0$. Graphically, this implies the marginal revenue schedule must decline more quickly than the marginal cost.

[2] For a discussion of the efforts made to measure the social cost of monopoly, see Posner (1975). He argues that much of the loss in consumer surplus that redounds to the monopolist is wasted by the firm on expenditures such as advertising designed to enhance or maintain monopoly status.

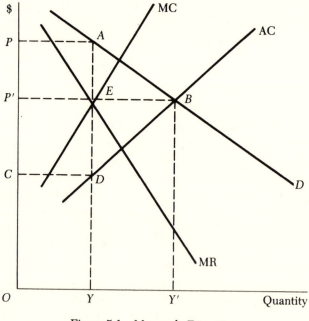

Figure 5.1   Monopoly Distortions

might not be attainable) but must be hypothesized. Lerner proposes an alternative measurement procedure. Assuming a constant cost industry, Y units of output would have been produced if average costs were $P'E$. The return above cost would then be $P'PAE$. Given pure competition in the product market, Y units would be produced only if the horizontal demand intersected MC at E. Factor rent would then be $CP'ED$, which Lerner refers to as monopsony revenue. We are able to measure these two effects, which together constitute monopoly revenue, without any reference to the cost and revenue schedules beyond Y.

Decreasing Cost Industries

The distortions associated with monopolies are particularly evident in the case of decreasing cost industries. Economies of scale may be sufficiently strong so that firms operate not on the upward-sloping portion of their average cost schedules but on the downward-sloping part. This may be the case for "natural" monopolies, those industries in which production is best achieved in a monopolistic rather than a competitive context. Electric light, water, telephone, and some other public utilities, if produced in a competitive market, would lead to excessive and unnecessary duplication of facilities and capital expenditures. The cost and revenue schedules for a decreasing cost industry are presented in Figure 5.2. They are constructed so that the second-order conditions for an extremum are fulfilled. Monopoly revenue will be maximized at *P* and *Y* but with the failure to realize many of the economies that would accompany increased production. Indeed, total costs are not being met; thus without some kind of support production would cease in the long run.

Sometimes monopolists may be able to extract large profits, while in other cases (decreasing cost) production may be less than society deems appropriate. As a consequence of these undesirable events, society has felt the need to impose rules on the operation of monopolies.

Forms of Regulation

In this section we examine policies that might be applied to a monopolistic industry to bring it closer to the competitive norm. The specific forms of such regulation are in practice quite complex, so only the basic issues involved will be discussed here.

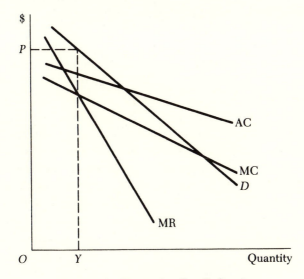

Figure 5.2   Decreasing Cost Industries

Antitrust Regulation

Antitrust regulation attempts to lessen the discretionary power of monopolists, thus rendering their demand schedules more horizontal. Such policies will be effective as long as monopolists derive their powers from practices designed to restrict competition. These we refer to as "artificial barriers"; they include restrictions of entry via patents, licensing or similar arrangements, control of raw material supplies, collusive agreements among producers, and others. On the other hand, when monopolists derive their power from something in the very nature of the product (i.e., goods requiring very large capital outlays, goods requiring physical connections for consumption, or goods with a small market relative to the efficient size of the facility), antitrust legislation will not prove effective. Some feel such legislation stifles entrepreneurial initiative, reduces the incentive for internally financed development, and is even anticapitalistic. Enforcement of such legislation is frequently administratively expensive and subject to the biases of alternative political administrations.

The first major piece of antimonopoly or antitrust legislation was the Sherman Act of 1890, which outlawed conspiracies or combinations in restraint of trade. Subsequent efforts to spell out more clearly the specific monopolistic practices deemed illegal led to the passage of the Clayton Act and the Federal Trade Commission Act, both in 1914. While monopolies "per se" were not illegal, certain of their actions aimed at lessening competition were unlawful.

The fundamental issue associated with all such legislation centers on how one could define competition. For many years the courts relied on the concentration of industry sales or assets among the major manufacturers as an index consistent with the Jeffersonian view that small is better than large. However, in industries where efficiency required firms large in size, serious problems arose. This conflict between competition defined by the number of firms in an industry and efficiency has yet to be resolved by the judicial system. It is clear that if the object of the courts is to promote economic welfare, then legal decisions must be based on economic efficiency, and the latter does not necessarily imply many firms. It is difficult to assess the impact of antitrust legislation, especially more recent legislation. Enforcement has varied with the courts and the political administration. Such legislation, however, has prevented overt collusion among participants in any one industry and made more difficult and less likely tacit agreements regarding price or output.

Price Regulation

While antitrust legislation attempts to create an environment more conducive to competition, price regulation directly imposes the government into the market. One might think of a pricing scheme analogous to that in the competitive model where price is set equal to marginal cost. However, as seen in Figure 5.2, pursuit of a marginal cost pricing policy might entail losses (AC < P) and the demise of the industry. Survival under such a pricing procedure would require government subsidization, and although consumers would benefit from lower prices and large outputs, they would be forced to bear the burden of the subsidy. With reference to Figure 5.1, marginal cost pricing would not completely eliminate profits, though it would lower price and increase output.

As an alternative, setting price equal to long-run average cost would preclude the need for subsidization, eliminate monopoly revenue, lower price, and increase output, as is obvious from Figure 5.2. Although the latter two changes would not be as large as in the previous case, given the direct cost of the subsidy and indirect costs of administration, such a scheme may be preferable to marginal cost pricing. Operationally, ascertaining a firm's average may be easier than ascertaining marginal cost. On the other hand, it may be argued that such procedures offer no incentive for firms to undertake the research and development necessary for technological advance.

To eliminate some of the problems associated with a direct pricing scheme, W. Baumol and A. Klevorick (1970)—among others—have proposed a rate-of-return regulation. Assume an output (Y) is produced at price P, with two variable inputs: capital (X_1) with price P_1 and labor (X_2) with an average wage of P_2. The rate-of-return constraint takes the form

$$\frac{PY - P_2X_2}{X_1} \leq s, \tag{5.1}$$

where s is the maximum allowable return on capital. For convenience, strict equality of (5.1) is assumed so that the profit-maximizing objective of the firm subject to (5.1) is:

$$\pi = PY - P_1X_1 - P_2X_2 + \lambda(sX_1 + P_2X_2 - PY). \tag{5.2}$$

Substituting the production function $f(X_1, X_2)$ in (5.2) and letting *MR* denote marginal revenue and MPP_i the marginal physical product of factor i, the first-order maximizing conditions are:

$$\frac{\partial \pi}{\partial X_1} = \text{MRMPP}_1 - P_1 + \lambda(s - \text{MRMPP}_1) = 0, \qquad (5.3)$$

$$\frac{\partial \pi}{\partial X_2} = \text{MRMPP}_2 - P_2 + \lambda(s - \text{MRMPP}_2) = 0, \qquad (5.4)$$

$$\frac{\partial \pi}{\partial \lambda} = sX_1 + P_2 X_2 - PY = 0. \qquad (5.5)$$

From (5.3) MR can be defined as:

$$\text{MR} = \frac{P_1 - \lambda s}{\text{MPP}_1(1 - \lambda)}. \qquad (5.3)'$$

The ratio of marginal physical products can be expressed as:

$$\frac{\text{MPP}_1}{\text{MPP}_2} = \frac{P_1 - \lambda s}{P_2(1 - \lambda)}. \qquad (5.4)'$$

Finally, adding and subtracting λP_1 from the right-hand numerator of (5.4)' yields:

$$\frac{\text{MPP}_1}{\text{MPP}_2} = \frac{P_1}{P_2} - \frac{\lambda(s - P_1)}{P_2(1 - \lambda)}. \qquad (5.6)$$

Assuming the rate of return s is above the price of capital P_1, then from (5.3) and (5.4), λ will be positive and less than one.[3] From (5.6) the ratio of marginal physical products will be less than the ratio of factor prices. Relative to the cost-minimizing-factor combinations, this implies a relative decrease (increase) in the marginal physical product of capital (labor). The result is a distortion in factor input proportions in the direction of greater capital intensity.

Peak Load Pricing

Until now we have assumed a uniform regulated price, but price setting may serve not only as a means of controlling monopoly revenue,

---

[3] The Lagrangian λ is the marginal profitability of increasing the allowable rate of return. One would clearly expect it to be positive but less than one.

but also as a device to alter consumption timing, thus reducing congestion. *Peak load* pricing is one of a number of multiple pricing schemes and is illustrative of such devices.

Let the total revenue of the monopolist equal the off-peak level of consumption (Y_o) times its price (P_o) plus the peak consumption level (Y_p) times its price (P_p). Costs are assumed at C_o in the off-peak period, and at C_o plus C_p in the peak period, where the latter term (C_p) varies with peak use. The profit (π) function may then be stated as:

$$\pi = P_o Y_o + P_p Y_p - C_o Y_o - C_o Y_p - C_p Y_p. \tag{5.7}$$

Assuming prices in each period are fixed, the first-order maximizing conditions are then:

$$P_o - C_o = 0, \tag{5.8}$$

$$P_p - C_o - C_p = 0. \tag{5.9}$$

In the off-peak period, price should equal marginal cost (C_o), while at peak times it should equal marginal cost (C_o) plus the additional cost associated with capacity utilization (C_p). Given the ability to expand, capacity cost $(C_p Y_p)$ could be eliminated and a single price (P_o) established. With fixed capacity, a simple price P_o or P_p would lead to either excessive losses or monopoly revenue.[4]

Regulation by Taxation

We can classify the many different tax schemes to control monopolies into two groups: those that do not affect either the price or output level of the monopolist and those that do. Lump-sum, profit, and corporate income taxes all reduce monopoly revenue but affect neither price nor quantity. To illustrate, consider the imposition of a tax at rate t on monopoly profits. Using the terminology defined earlier, the objective function is:

$$\pi = PY - CY - t(PY - CY). \tag{5.10}$$

As is obvious, the first-order profit-maximizing conditions are the same as in the absence of the tax. With reference to Figure 5.1, the effect of

---

[4] Implicit in our discussion are a number of simplifying assumptions and a more complete analysis may be found in P. Steiner (1957) or O. E. Williamson (1966).

such taxes is to shift the average cost curve upward with no change in any other schedule. Analysis of the effects of a lump-sum tax is left to the reader.

Sales taxes, which may be "ad valorem" (a percentage of the sales price) or a unit tax (a given amount per unit product), have the effect of raising prices and decreasing output. Assume a specific tax of α dollars is imposed. The objective function now becomes:

$$\pi = PY - CY - \alpha Y. \tag{5.11}$$

The first-order maximizing condition is then:

$$MR = MC + \alpha. \tag{5.12}$$

To the marginal cost schedule must be added an amount equal to α. Obviously, the effect of such an action on the price and quantity of Y demanded will be determined by the price elasticity of demand (η). Whether such policies bring us closer to a social optimum cannot be answered in the abstract. Clearly, however, both the level of resources devoted to production of this good and its consumption decline. The more inelastic the demand the greater the ability of the monopolist to shift the burden or incidence of the tax on to the consumer. It is important to keep in mind that our discussion was premised on profit maximization by the monopolist. If the firm adopts some other objective, such as *mark-up pricing* where a fixed return above cost is maintained, then under all forms of taxation it may be able to shift the burden to the consumer.

Interindustry Distortions

Until now we have focused on the effects of regulation within a given industry. The effects in one industry, however, are likely to influence conditions in other sectors as well. The corporate income tax is a tax on capital income arising in a particular firm or industry. One effect of the tax is likely to be a reallocation of capital into tax-free sectors, reducing capital intensity where the tax is in effect. Similarly, taxes governing depreciation, capital gains, deductibility of expenses, and many other factors are likely to generate both intra- and interindustry resource reallocations.

Public Ownership or Operation

The previously mentioned forms of regulation may be inappropriate for some monopolies because of the excessive profits or losses to firms or consumers that may result. In such circumstances, the government may choose to take over provision of the good through direct ownership or operation, or via some form of semipublic corporation. The Tennessee Valley Authority (TVA) and the Communications Satellite Corporation (COMSAT) are two examples of the latter. Mail service is an example of direct ownership and operation.

In these cases come objective other than profit maximization must be formulated. The necessary first-order conditions for efficiency must then be derived in light of this objective and all related constraints. The need for such direct control will increase as the divergence between the objectives of the firm and the collective objective grows. Those individuals and groups arguing for a national health care program do so under the premise that private operation of the health care industry is not consistent with social welfare maximization.

Second Best

In some cases regulation of the sector violating the Pareto conditions may not be possible or feasible. Imperfections may exist in so many sectors that administrative costs render such policies impractical. The question then arises as to what should be done in those sectors that can be controlled when the rest of the economy is not competitive.

A number of people discovered, but Lipsey and Lancaster (1956–57) formulated most precisely, that the Paretian conditions may not be valid criteria for welfare maximization when they cannot be simultaneously met in every sector of the economy. A "piecemeal" approach, where efforts are made to satisfy the marginal requirements in as many sectors as possible, is not necessarily in the best social interest. The issue is, if the Pareto conditions cannot be satisfied everywhere, what should be done to realize a "second best" solution? The term "second best" was coined by James Meade in his classic work *Trade and Welfare* (1955). Ozza (1955) investigates a market with tariffs, Viner (1950) the effects of customs unions, and Little (1951) and Meade (1955) the influence of taxes. We will limit the discussion to monopoly.

Theories of Second Best

Our objective is utility (U) maximization, which is determined by the level of goods produced and consumed $(Y_1, \ldots, Y_n)$. We are constrained by the production function for these goods and the available resources in the economy $(\overline{X}_1, \ldots, \overline{X}_m)$. The production function in implicit form can be expressed as:

$$F(Y_1, \ldots, Y_n, \overline{X}_1, \ldots, \overline{X}_m) = 0. \tag{5.13}$$

Using the Lagrangian technique and deriving the first-order conditions yields:

$$L = U(Y_1, \ldots Y_n) + \lambda F(Y_1, \ldots Y_n, \overline{X}_1, \ldots, \overline{X}_m), \tag{5.14}$$

$$\frac{\partial L}{\partial Y_i} = \frac{\partial U}{\partial Y_i} + \lambda \frac{\partial F}{\partial Y_i} = 0, \qquad i = 1, \ldots, n, \tag{5.15}$$

$$\frac{\partial L}{\partial \lambda} = F(Y_1, \ldots, Y_n, X_1, \ldots, \overline{X}_m) = 0. \tag{5.16}$$

Maximization implies from (5.15) that the ratios of marginal utilities or rates of commodity substitution for every pair of goods equal the ratios of their marginal costs.

For one particular good (Y_1), it is now assumed that (5.15) cannot be satisfied. Instead:

$$\frac{\partial U}{\partial Y_1} - k \frac{\partial F}{\partial Y_1} = 0, \qquad \text{where } k \neq \lambda. \tag{5.17}$$

Reformulating the Lagrangian function with this additional constraint yields:

$$L = U(Y_1, \ldots, Y_n) + \lambda F(Y_1, \ldots Y_n, \overline{X}_1, \ldots, \overline{X}_m) \tag{5.18}$$

$$+ \mu \left(\frac{\partial U}{\partial Y_1} - k \frac{\partial F}{\partial Y_1} \right).$$

The first-order conditions now become:

$$\frac{\partial L}{\partial Y_i} = \frac{\partial U}{\partial Y_i} + \lambda \frac{\partial F}{\partial Y_i} + \mu \left(\frac{\partial \dfrac{\partial U}{\partial Y_1}}{\partial Y_i} - k \frac{\partial \dfrac{\partial F}{\partial Y_1}}{\partial Y_i} \right) = 0, \quad (5.19)$$

$$i = 1, \ldots, n,$$

$$\frac{\partial L}{\partial \lambda} = F(Y_1, \ldots, Y_n, \overline{X}_1, \ldots, \overline{X}_m) = 0, \quad (5.20)$$

$$\frac{\partial L}{\partial \mu} = \left(\frac{\partial U}{\partial Y_1} - k \frac{\partial F}{\partial Y_1} \right) = 0. \quad (5.21)$$

The following will be helpful in interpreting (5.19): $\partial U / \partial Y_i$ is the marginal utility of i (MU_i); $\partial F / \partial Y_i$ is the marginal cost of i (MC_i); $\partial (\partial U / \partial Y_1) / \partial Y_i$ is the effect of i on the marginal utility of Y_1 (the cross-order partial MU_{1i}); $\partial (\partial F / \partial Y_1) / \partial Y_i$ is the effect of i on the marginal cost of Y_1 (the cross-order partial MC_{1i}). Equation (5.19) thus implies for any two commodities i and j:

$$RCS_{ij} = \frac{MU_i}{MU_j} = \frac{MC_i \lambda + \mu(MU_{1i} - kMC_{1i})}{MC_j \lambda + \mu(MU_{1j} - kMC_{1j})}. \quad (5.22)$$

If Y_1 did not affect either the marginal utility or cost of Y_i or Y_j, then the terms in parentheses in (5.22) would equal zero. Satisfying the Pareto conditions for all commodities but Y_1 would then be consistent with maximizing (5.18). A "piecemeal" or partial equilibrium approach that considers each sector separately would, only in that case, be consistent with utility maximization.

Additive Separability

The cross-order effects MU_{ij} and MC_{ij} for all i and j ($i \neq j$) will be zero when the utility functions and production functions are respectively additively separable. A function of the form $F(X_1, \ldots, X_n)$ is additively separable if it can be expressed as $f_1(X_1) + \ldots + f_n(X_n)$, thus ensuring that the cross-order partial derivatives are zero.

In many cases it may be argued that goods are sufficiently unrelated—that the cross-order effects are insignificant. Peanut and automobile production may be such that neither the marginal utility nor the marginal cost of one is significantly altered by changes in consumption or production of the other. Only if such were the case would a partial equilibrium approach be acceptable.

Conditions for Second Best

Equations (5.19), (5.20), and (5.21) are the necessary first-order conditions when there is an impediment to the realization of the Pareto conditions. They are "second best" in the sense that the value of the objective function will be less than if the impediment did not exist and the Paretian conditions were met. They are, however, the necessary first-order conditions for maximizing this new system. When additional constraints such as (5.17) are introduced, the second-order conditions become more complicated, and the existence of a solution to the problem becomes more difficult to demonstrate.

As economies grow and expand, sectors tend to become more interdependent. In such circumstances the relatively straightforward Pareto conditions may possibly be approximated but not the requirements of "second best." One may thus be forced into a choice of no policy at all or a "piecemeal" Pareto approach.

An Example: Pricing in a Nationalized Industry

The illustration we consider is the same as that used by Lipsey and Lancaster in their earlier-mentioned article. Assume an economy producing three goods, Y_1, Y_2, and Y_3, with a fixed endowment of resources $\bar{X}$. Industry Y_1 is monopolized, Y_2 is nationalized, and Y_3 is competitive. Our goal is to find the optimal pricing policy in the nationalized sector consistent with utility maximization.

The monopolist will set a price greater than marginal cost so that:

$$\text{RCS}_{13} \equiv \frac{P_1}{P_3} \equiv \frac{\text{MU}_1}{\text{MU}_3} > \frac{\text{MC}_1}{\text{MC}_3} = \text{RPT}_{13}.$$

Letting k be a constant greater than one, we can rewrite the above as:

$$\text{MU}_1\text{MC}_3 = k\,\text{MU}_3\text{MC}_1. \qquad (5.17)'$$

This represents the additional constraint due to the market imperfection. Again assuming an implicit production function and utility maximization, the objective function may be expressed as:

$$L = U(Y_1, Y_2, Y_3) + \lambda F(Y_1, Y_2, Y_3, \overline{X}) + \mu(MU_1 MC_3 - k MU_3 MC_1). \qquad (5.18)'$$

The first-order conditions are then:

$$\frac{\partial L}{\partial Y_i} = MU_i + \lambda MC_i + \mu(MU_{1i} MC_{3i} - k\ MU_{3i} MC_{1i}) = 0, \qquad i = 1,2,3,$$

$$(5.19)'$$

$$\frac{\partial L}{\partial \lambda} = F(Y_1, Y_2, Y_3, \overline{X}) = 0, \qquad\qquad (5.20)'$$

$$\frac{\partial L}{\partial \mu} = MU_1 MC_3 - k MU_3 MC_1 = 0. \qquad\qquad (5.21)'$$

With reference to the competitive sector, from (5.19)' the appropriate pricing policy for Y_2 relative to the competitive price (P_3) is:

$$\frac{P_2}{P_3} = \frac{MC_2 \lambda + \mu(MU_{12} MC_{32} - k MU_{32} MC_{12})}{MC_3 \lambda + \mu(MU_{13} MC_{33} - k MU_{33} MC_{13})}. \qquad (5.22)'$$

The rather formidable terms enclosed in the parentheses measure (1) the interdependencies of Y_2 on the utility and cost of Y_1 and Y_3 (the numerator) and (2) the effect of Y_3 on its own utility and cost, and the utility and cost of Y_1 (the denominator). The cross-order partial MU_{ij} will be positive if the goods are complements in consumption and negative if substitutes. MC_{ij} will be positive if i and j are substitutes in production and negative if they are complements.

What to Do? (Third Best)

Until now we have assumed that the distortion existed in one sector only. Obviously, when there are many distortions, the constraints and their complexity grow to a degree that practical application of the above analysis is impossible. Crucial in the implementation of such policies is the cost and availability of information. Complexity and lack of information may leave little alternative to the Pareto "first best" strategy. Meade (1955) makes the additional point that "second best" policies are likely to bring about significant changes in the distribution of income relative to that associated with a "first best" approach. While ensuring efficiency, it might not ensure optimal welfare measured in terms of equity.

Summary

Two general approaches are possible to alleviate market distortions. On the one hand are policies directed toward the offending sector; on the other are offsetting policies aimed at related sectors. Distortions introduce additional constraints and render the maximizing conditions more complicated. In many cases the absence of sufficient information makes infeasible implementation of second-best methodologies, and, in such circumstances, a first-best approach may be the only alternative. While thus far we have restricted our discussion to market imperfections, distortions may also arise because of the nature and characteristics of a particular good. The next chapters will explore these issues and suggest possible corrective actions.

References

Baumol, W., and A. Klevorick. 1970. "Input Theories and Rate of Return Regulation." *Bell Journal of Economics* 1 (Autumn):162–90.

Harberger, A. C. 1974. *Taxation and Welfare*. Boston: Little, Brown.

Lerner, A. P. 1933–34. "The Concept of Monopoly and the Measurement of Monopoly Power." *Review of Economic Studies* I:157–75.

Lipsey, R. G., and K. Lancaster. 1956–57. "The General Theory of Second Best." *Review of Economic Studies* 24:11–22.

Little, I. M. D. 1951. "Direct versus Indirect Taxes," *The Economic Journal.* 61:577–84.

McManus, M. 1958–59. "Comments on the 'The General Theory of Second Best.' " *Review of Economic Studies* 26:209–24.

Meade, J. E. 1955. *Trade and Welfare*. London: Oxford University Press.

Ng, Y. -K. 1980. *Welfare Economics*. New York: John Wiley.

Ozza, S. A. 1955. "An Essay in the Theory of Tariffs." *Journal of Political Economy* 63:489–99.

Posner, R. A. 1975. "The Social Cost of Monopoly and Regulation." *Journal of Political Economy* 83:807–27.

Steiner, P. 1957. "Peak Loads and Efficiency Pricing." *Quarterly Journal of Economics* 71:585–610.

Viner, J. 1950. *The Customs Union Issue*. New York: Carnegie Endowment for International Peace.

Williamson, O. E. 1966. "Peak-Load Pricing and Optimal Capacity under Indivisibility Constraints." *American Economic Review* 56:810–27.

Winch, D. M. 1921. *Analytical Welfare Economics*. Harmondsworth: Penguin Books Ltd.

Supplementary Readings

Averch, H., and L. Johnson. 1962. "Behavior of the Firm under Regulatory Constraint." *American Economic Review* 52:1052–69.

Baumol, W., and D. Bradford. 1970. "Optimal Departures from Marginal Cost Pricing." *American Economic Review* 60:265–83.

Lipsey, R. G. and K. Lancaster. 1958–59. "McManus on Second Best," *Review of Economic Studies* 26:225–6.

Westfield, F. 1971. "Methodology of Evaluating Economic Regulation." *American Economic Review, Proceedings* 61:211–17.

Chapter 6

EXTERNALITIES AND PUBLIC GOODS

Until now we have not made any distinction between the private valuation of goods and services and the social valuation. In this chapter we consider cases where these need not be the same. We will also discuss how such differences alter the conditions necessary for optimality. Our point of departure is, to devise a spectrum for classifying goods: at one end are "pure private goods" and at the other "pure public goods."

Pure Private Goods

A pure private good is one for which there is *rivalry* in consumption. In other words, a private good is one that many consumers desire, but consumption by one precludes consumption by others. Many people desire steak, but consumption by one person prevents consumption of that steak by another. Rivalry or competitiveness in consumption is inherent in the very nature of the good. You and I compete for consumption of the steak because if you consume it I cannot. On the other hand, we both may desire to use a local swimming pool, but my use of the pool does not rival yours since we can share the facility without disutility to either of us.

Goods for which there is no rivalry may become private by virtue of the ability to practice exclusion. It may happen that you can exclude me from using the swimming pool. You may have ownership or *property rights*, or you may be able to use force to prevent my use. In the steak example, my consumption excludes you because of the nature of the good. The right to practice exclusion arises when I pay the purchase price of the steak, thus rendering it my property. Because the good became my property on purchase, I would be willing to pay a price equal to its marginal benefit (utility) to me. Since I alone would consume the good, the social benefit and the private benefit would be one and the same. The price would equal the marginal benefit and marginal cost of the good.

The distinction in the literature between the notions of *rivalry* and *exclusion* is ambiguous. The former ensures exclusion by consumption due to the nature of the good. The latter is the right or ability to exclude arising primarily out of the system of contracts and property rights. Both are necessary for the equivalence of private and social valuations. In addition, both properties are assumed in the derivation of the Pareto conditions.

Pure Public Goods

A pure public good is one for which there is no rivalry in consumption. The opportunity cost of consumption is zero so that my consumption in no way precludes you. Arrow (1962) refers to this as the "indivisibility" property. The marginal benefit of such a good would be the benefit to all those who partake of the good. While the steak could be divided among individuals, each deriving a separate benefit, the swimming pool is shared as a unit. The marginal cost pricing rule implicit in a competitive market would dictate a zero price for pure public goods. Such a policy would render impossible production of the good by the private sector since even though the marginal cost of consumption is zero, the marginal cost of production will, in all probability, not be zero.

National defense protection is frequently cited as an example of a public good. Within reasonable limits, the opportunity cost of providing a given level of defense protection to citizens of a country will not increase as the population does. Individuals do not rival one another for protection. The value of this protection to any person may be quite small while the value to society is quite large. It is obviously very difficult to establish property or ownership rights to this good. You are unable to purchase for your exclusive protection a certain number of units of national defense, but it is nonrivalry, not nonexcludability, that constitutes the essence of "publicness." Let's return to our earlier swimming pool example. The opportunity cost of allowing an additional person to use the pool is zero; therefore, we should not charge that person to use the pool. From this point of view, this is a public good. Unlike national defense, I may own the pool and thereby have the legal right to exclude others. But, even though I have the right, it would be inefficient to exercise it.

The term "public good" is sometimes applied to goods or services that are in some sense collectively or communally owned or provided even though not all such goods are public in the sense defined above. The postal service, education, and the railroads are not strictly public, but the government plays a principal role in their provision. Although the government may provide other goods, because of the nature of public goods, they must be collectively produced. The private sector could replace the postal service, but it would be much less likely to provide an adequate level of defense.

Publicness

Obviously, there are all different degrees of rivalry and excludability in consumption. My consumption of classical music may not preclude you from also enjoying it, depending on how high the volume of my stereo is. It may rival your consumption of rock music, however. Since the ability to establish property rights differs among goods, so also will exclusion. While land surface can be partitioned and titles established, can the same be done to the sea, and to what's above and below the earth's surface?

Most goods are neither "pure" public or "pure" private but somewhere in between. The same good may tend to be public under one set of conditions (i.e., a swimming pool with considerable underutilization) and private under another (i.e., the same pool at or over full capacity). In subsequent discussions it will be helpful to assume we can divide goods precisely. Our discussion of *externalities* permits consideration of intermediate cases.

Market Demand Curves

The property of nonrivalry in consumption has implications for the derivation of the market demand curve. For a private good the aggregate or market demand is the *horizontal* summation of each consumer's demand. At any given price we would find the sum of the quantities consumed by each individual. The market demand for a public good is found by adding individual demand schedules *vertically*. For any given quantity we want the collective valuation or willingness to pay. This is found by adding together how much each consumer is willing to pay for the same quantity consumed by each and every individual.

Optimality in the Provision of Public Goods

Since the private sector would not provide public goods, such goods must be produced under the direction of some collective body. Our discussion of the problem follows the classic treatment by Samuelson (1955). Other approaches are available, and the interested reader may consult Musgrave and Musgrave (1973).

Consider a simple two-person economy producing a private good Y_1, of which Y_{11} is consumed by consumer 1 and Y_{21} by consumer 2. Total consumption is then $Y_1 = Y_{11} + Y_{21}$. A public good Y_2 is equally available to all consumers so that $Y_2 = Y_{12} = Y_{22}$. Figure 6.1a and b represent the indifference curves of consumer 1 and 2, respectively, with Y_1 measured vertically and Y_2 horizontally. The production possibilities curve for the provision of Y_1 and Y_2 is denoted PP in Figure 6.1c. Adopting the Pareto criterion that any reallocation that increases at least one person's utility is desirable, we can proceed as follows. Choose a utility level for 2, U_2^1 on indifference curve CD. Plotting this curve in 6.1c permits us to find for any level of Y_2 the amount of Y_1 available to consumer 1, with consumer 2 maintaining U_2^1 utility, measured as the vertical distance between CD and PP. Plotting these points in 6.1a as $C'D'$ yields the opportunity locus of 1 given U_2^1. Consumer 1 will maximize utility at the point of tangency between the opportunity locus and, in this case, indifference curve U_1^1. Consumption by 1 will be Y_{11}^E and Y_{12}^E of the private and public goods, respectively. This implies total production of the public good will also be Y_{12}^E, and from 6.1c total production of the private good will be Y_1^E.

Consumer 1 will be at E_1 and 2 at E_2, and it is impossible to increase the utility of one participant given that of the other. This process could be repeated for every utility level of 2. The locus of utility combinations consistent with the Pareto criterion is denoted BB in Figure 6.1d, where the utility of consumer 2 is measured vertically and that of 1, horizontally. Given a Bergson-Samuelson social welfare function, optimality will occur at Ω in Figure 6.1d.

The necessary optimality conditions can be seen more clearly by letting Y_1 represent a common denominator or *numeraire*. The slope of

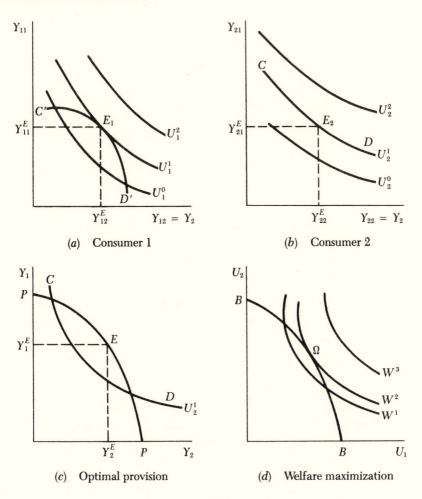

(a) Consumer 1

(b) Consumer 2

(c) Optimal provision

(d) Welfare maximization

Figure 6.1 Public Goods

the production possibilities curve (PP) expressed positively is then the marginal cost of producing Y_2. We will refer to it as the marginal social cost represented by MSC in Figure 6.2. Given indifference curve CD for 2, the rate of commodity substitution can be thought of as the price of Y_2 by consumer 2 measured in terms of Y_1. The relationship between Y_2 and its price is represented as RCS_{22} in Figure 6.2. From U_1^1 in Figure 6.1a, the demand for Y_2 by consumer 1 can be derived and is labeled RCS_{12}. Since Y_2 is a public good, the market demand can be found by adding RCS_{12} and RCS_{22}. The intersection of ΣRCS and MSC corresponds to the level of output Y_2^E. Note that this need not coincide

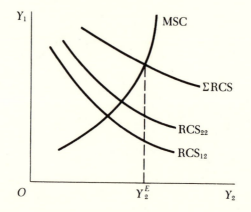

Figure 6.2   Demand and Supply of Public Goods

with Ω in 6.1d since the latter implies some assessment of the distribution of utilities between consumers.

Mathematical Restatement

Additional insight into the nature of the problem may be obtained by formulating it with the method of Lagrange. The objective is to maximize the utility of consumer 1 given a level of utility for consumer 2 and a production possibilities function. The latter will be expressed in implicit form where the fixed supply of resources is denoted $\overline{X}$. The objective function and first-order maximizing conditions are then:

$$L = U_1(Y_{11}, Y_2) + \lambda F(Y_1, Y_2, \overline{X}) + \mu[U_2(Y_{21}, Y_2) - U_2^1], \tag{6.1}$$

$$\frac{\partial L}{\partial Y_{11}} = \frac{\partial U_1}{\partial Y_{11}} + \lambda \frac{\partial F}{\partial Y_1} = 0, \tag{6.2}$$

$$\frac{\partial L}{\partial Y_2} = \frac{\partial U_1}{\partial Y_2} + \lambda \frac{\partial F}{\partial Y_2} + \mu \frac{\partial U_2}{\partial Y_2} = 0, \tag{6.3}$$

$$\frac{\partial L}{\partial \lambda} = F(Y_1, Y_2, \overline{X}) = 0, \tag{6.4}$$

$$\frac{\partial L}{\partial \mu} = U_2(Y_{21}, Y_2) - U_2^1 = 0. \tag{6.5}$$

Expressing (6.3) and (6.2) as a ratio, the partial derivatives of the utility function as marginal utilities (MU), and the partials with respect to the production function as marginal costs (MC) yields:

$$\frac{MC_2}{MC_1} = \frac{MU_{12} + \mu MU_{22}}{MU_{11}}. \tag{6.6}$$

The Lagrangian for above (μ) converts the marginal utility of consumer 2 into a form additive with that of consumer 1.[1]

Equation (6.6) points out an interesting paradox since it implies an interpersonal utility comparison embodied in μ, while at the same time being the Pareto condition that avoided such comparisons in the case of private goods. While it is true we could attempt to solve for μ, the resultant conditions become extremely complex. This problem of having to express the Pareto conditions in terms of interpersonal comparisons will arise whenever the same good enters into the utility function of more than one consumer. This is in the very nature of a public good, but it also occurs, as we will see, with goods having degrees of "publicness."

Mechanisms for the Provision of Public Goods

Although the analysis by Samuelson yields the Pareto optimal amount of the public good, the issue still remains as to how it will be produced since once in existence its price should be zero. Analogous to a private good, one might think of setting a uniform price to cover production costs, but those deriving a benefit less than the price would cease consumption. Since their consumption is costless, this deprivation would be unnecessary, and it would increase the price to those that continued to consume. Alternatively, we could think of charging each individual a price equal to the marginal benefit derived from use. The result, called a "Lindahl equilibrium," is analogous to the assumption the price is set by a perfect price discriminator. Although this marginal price equals marginal benefit approach solves the problem associated with uniform pricing, it creates an incentive for deception. By understating the benefit derived from consumption, you lower the price that must be paid. The incentive is to be a *free-rider*—to reap the

---

[1] The Lagrangian multiplier in this case is a measure of the marginal effect of a change in consumer 2's utility on consumer 1. It allows us to add the utilities of consumers.

benefits while letting others pay the cost. The issue, then, is how can we accurately assess individual preferences on the basis of which charges or fees can be affixed?

Answers to this very difficult question have been given by Vickrey (1961), Clarke (1971, 1972), and Groves (1973) and will be briefly summarized here. Each consumer is asked to pay a fraction (s_i) of the total production cost of the public good $(\Sigma_i s_i = 1)$. The fractions may be equal or arrived at through some mutual agreement. Ignoring aggregation problems, the market demand is found by adding each consumer's demand vertically. We will denote it as DD in Figure 6.3a, where units of the public good Y_2 are measured horizontally. Assuming a constant cost industry, the average (AC) and marginal (MC) cost curves will be horizontal in Figure 6.3a, and Y_2^A units of the good should be provided.

In addition to the fraction s_i of total cost, each consumer must also pay a "Clarke-Groves" tax. Letting per unit cost equal 1, MC $- s_j$ represents the MC to all individuals other than j and is denoted MC$_{i \neq j}$ in Figure 6.3a. Analogously, $D_{i \neq j}$ is the aggregate demand excluding j. In Figure 6.3a, they intersect at Y_2^B, a level of output less than previously.[2] The tax on consumer j is the difference between MC$_{i \neq j}$ and $D_{i \neq j}$ from Y_2^B to Y_2^A (BCE). The triangle BCE is the loss to other consumers because of j's preferences, and j is asked to bear the cost of this loss. Tideman and Tullock (1976) summarize the process in the phrase "entitlement to the consequence of one's abstention." This exercise could be repeated for each consumer to arrive at a set of appropriate taxes.

To show more clearly the irrationality of deception in this scheme, we present the demand by j (D_j) in Figure 6.3b. To find j's tax, we calculate the difference between the cost ($\$1$) and the aggregate willingness to pay by others $(D - D_j)$ at every quantity. This schedule is labeled ss_j in Figure 6.3b and is the mirror image of $D - D_j$. We assume at Y_2^B, j has a greater demand than his cost share so that including his demand increases the quantity. Such, however, need not be the case. Viewing ss_j as j's supply schedule, the intersection of demand and supply is at the optimal quantity Y_2^A. The cost to j is the standard payment s_j, whether he consumes or not, plus the Clarke-Groves tax LMN. This is the amount that would have to be paid to individuals other than j to make them indifferent between Y_2^A and Y_2^B.

If the consumer j understated his demand, he would lose part of the

---

[2] Such need not be the case. The demand schedule could be drawn so that $Y_2^B > Y_2^A$. In this case the tax would equal $D_{i \neq j} - $ MC$_{i \neq j}$.

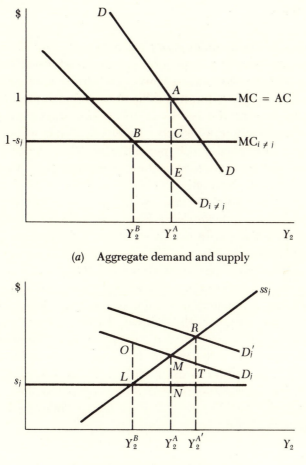

(a) Aggregate demand and supply

(b) Individual demand and supply

Figure 6.3   Financing Public Goods

surplus *LMO*. If he overstates his demand at say D_j' and the quantity $Y_2^{A'}$, his additional taxes would be $Y_2^A Y_2^{A'} RM$, while the gain would be $Y_2^A Y_2^{A'} TM$. In neither case is there a gain from incorrectly stating one's preferences. The case where the benefit is less than the tax share is left as an exercise. The revenue derived from the tax represents a surplus above cost, and it is assumed to be wasted. If individuals were to benefit from the surplus, and this consideration is taken into account, then profitable deceptions may arise.[3]

---

[3] For a further discussion of cases where the Clarke-Groves tax does not lead to Pareto optimal results, see Hurwicz (1972).

Externalities

The analysis above assumes goods are either pure public or pure private. In many situations, as previously mentioned, the distinction may not be as clear cut. Purchasing flowers and shrubs to beautify my yard may be a private good, but it is difficult to exclude others from taking pleasure in viewing the results or to exclude surrounding property from any appreciation my efforts may entail. Goods whose consumption by one individual affects persons other than the principal consumer are said to have externalities in consumption. Goods whose production by one firm affects other individuals or firms are said to have externalities in production.[4] Externalities are *spill over* or *third person* effects on individuals or firms other than those directly involved. If benefits accrue to others, the externalities are positive; if harm or damages are inflicted, they are negative.

Externalities arise because of nonexcludability that may be due to nonrivalry in consumption or the absence of property rights. A firm's research and development program may generate new knowledge that is usable by other firms in the industry. One firm's use of this knowledge does not prevent or rival its use by others. The steel mill can pollute the air because the air is a "free" good. No one has a property right to air, so the firm can use it without paying any cost. The more significant the externalities associated with a good, the less private and more public the good becomes, as a model developed by J. Buchanan (1965) will make clear.

Buchanan's Model of Externalities

We will now introduce as arguments into the utility function not only the amounts of goods consumed but also the number of consumers sharing in the consumption. Y_{ij} will be the amount of commodity j consumed by i, and N_{ij} the total number of individuals who share Y_j with i. In the case of a pure private good, N_{ij} will be 1, and for pure public goods, approach infinity. The utility function in our simple two-good, two-consumer economy will be:

---

[4] Some would argue that all externalities arise by virtue of consumption since without demand goods would not be produced. Pollution generated by steel production could be viewed as a consumption externality associated with steel consumption. It should be kept in mind that the distinction between production and consumption is not always obvious.

$$U_i = U_i[(Y_{i1},N_{i1})(Y_{i2},N_{i2})], \qquad i = 1,2. \tag{6.7}$$

The marginal utilities associated with additional participants in consumption $(\partial U_i/\partial N_{ij})$ may be positive or negative. You may prefer that there be more than you alone on the tennis court. On the other hand, too many people may lead to congestion and disutility. Individuals are assumed to be homogeneous and share equally in the good and its cost. Transaction costs are zero as are exclusion costs, and discrimination is impossible.

The production function in implicit form will analogously be expressed as:

$$F[(Y_{i1},N_{i1}),(Y_{i2},N_{i2}),\overline{X}]; \qquad i = 1,2, \tag{6.8}$$

where $\overline{X}$ refers to the level of resources in the economy. Production now becomes dependent on the size of the consuming unit as well as the level of output. It is reasonable to assume that for any level or size facility, marginal cost will vary with the number of users. The marginal cost of accommodating one more in the swimming pool depends on the number using the pool (i.e., greater use may imply improved water purification systems, etc.).

Maximization of (6.7) subject to (6.8) will, as is obvious, require equality between the rates of commodity substitution for all consumers and each pair of commodities with the ratio of marginal costs for each pair of commodities. It will also require that the ratio of marginal utilities for each pair of goods associated with incrementing the size of the consuming unit equal the ratio of marginal costs such increments entail. Or,

$$\frac{MU_{i1}(N_1)}{MU_{i2}(N_2)} = \frac{MC_1(N_1)}{MC_2(N_2)}, \qquad i = 1,2, \tag{6.9}$$

where the (N) indicates the partials are taken with respect to the size of the variable.

The above analysis assumes there is discretionary power over both the level of consumption and production and also over the unit size. In many cases the consumer or the firm may not be able to determine the size of the sharing unit. An individual consumer will probably not be able to regulate the number of users of a public swimming pool, and even the provider of the pool may have only incomplete control.

The conditions for optimality may be seen more clearly with the help of Figure 6.4. In 6.4*a*, the cost and benefits per person associated with various quantities of *Y* (sizes of a swimming pool) are reported. The subscripts of these curves indicate the size of the sharing unit (*N*). Two representative sets of schedules are reported for $N = 1$ and k. In 6.4*b*, the quantity of *Y* is fixed, denoted by the subscripts 1 and *n*, but the size of the sharing unit varies. Again, cost and benefits per person are measured.[5]

From 6.4*a*, one can map out the locus of points where marginal cost of *Y* is equal to the marginal benefit. This will give the optimal quantity of *Y* for various *N*. It is represented as *AA* in 6.4*c*. *BB* similarly from 6.4*b* measures the optimal sharing unit (*N*) given *Y*. It is derived from the tangency points of the cost and benefit schedules, indicating sizes of the sharing unit for given levels of *Y* at which marginal costs and benefits are equal. The coordinates of *Q* will determine the optimal level of *Y* and participants in consumption. Without restrictions on the number of commodities and participants, there is no assurance that a solution either exists or is unique. Nor, without similar restrictions, can we be assured there is a dynamic leading to *Q*.[6]

Theory of Clubs

Buchanan's model is one of a series of efforts to arrive at optimality conditions for private goods with externalities, or what are sometimes called impure public goods—that is, goods with a nonzero marginal cost of consumption. The concept of a "club" embodies the idea of a voluntary group of individuals sharing in the consumption and possibly cost of some good or service. By focusing on a representative utility function, average net benefits are maximized.

The analysis has been extended to the entire economy in which the welfare of both club members and nonmembers is maximized subject to constraints on production and distribution.[7] Three issues are

---

[5] The cost and benefit curves may assume any of a number of forms. In 6.4*a* it is assumed that for very small sharing units costs exceed benefits. As the sharing unit increases for a given facility size, costs per person decline since they can be spread over more individuals. Benefits will increase until congestion occurs.

[6] Assume we are at N' to the right of N^Q. The optimal *Y* can be found from *AA* as Y'. From *BB* for Y' optimal *N* moves toward N^Q. A mechanism seems to exist that would move the system to *Q*. Assume we begin at N'' with an optimal *Y* of Y'', will there again be a tendency to move to *Q*? What if we began by choosing *Y* rather than *N*?

[7] For an excellent survey of the literature see T. Sandler and J. T. Tschirhart, "The Economic Theory of Clubs: An Evaluative Survey," *Journal of Economic Literature* 18 (December 1980):1481–1521.

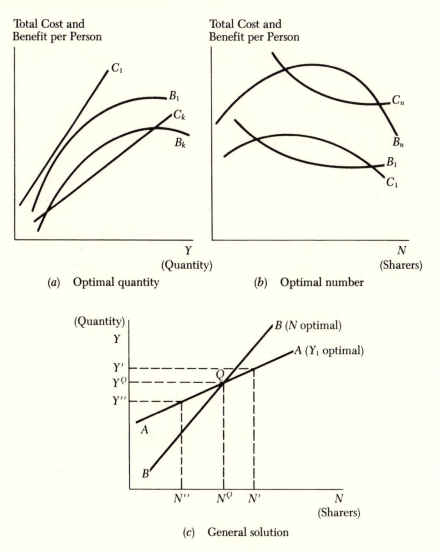

(a) Optimal quantity

(b) Optimal number

(c) General solution

Figure 6.4 Public Goods

involved: the optimal quantity of the good, the optimal number of participants in its consumption, and the pricing or toll structure compatible with the realization of optimality. In addition, the effects of membership heterogeneity, discrimination, exclusion costs, and alternative specifications of the crowding functions have also been examined. On the other hand, only cursory attention has been given to the effects of transaction costs.

The theory of clubs has been applied to many problems both within economics and in the broader area of collective decision making. In concert with a pricing structure not unlike the Clarke-Groves tax, it has been proposed as a method for regulating decreasing cost public utilities. It was pointed out earlier that, under such circumstances, marginal cost pricing is inappropriate because prices would be less than average cost. By imposing a pricing structure consisting of a license fee and a usage fee, utilization of the facility (club size) can be controlled while, at the same time, ensuring an adequate return.

Some very early studies by Walters (1961) and Mohring and Mitchell (1962) applied the analysis to highway usage and the resultant congestion costs. C. Cicchetti and V. K. Smith (1976) examined the appropriate membership for a recreational area. Tiebout (1956) uses a model of clubs to determine the appropriate size of local governing jurisdictions. Efficiency in the provision of combinations of various public goods can be realized by individuals "voting with the feet." Optimality occurs when the community is at the size that minimizes the cost per person of providing a package of public goods. Communities with low costs will attract residents, while individuals will leave high-cost areas.

Game Theory—Alternative Methodology

In Chapter 2, when we derived the Pareto optimal conditions it was assumed that each person acted independently. That subset of the loci of Pareto optimal positions such that no individual could improve his position by any coalition constituted the *core*. The appropriate size of a sharing unit can be thought of as the optimizing coalition, and its determination is referred to as *game theory*. The set of outcomes in a game theoretic problem is the net gains from coalitions of players. Although the traditional approach allows us to arrive at a relative price scheme from the first-order conditions, the game theory approach does not, thus representing a serious shortcoming.

Summary

Goods can be divided into groups on the basis of the number of individuals that can consume the good without adversely affecting the ability of others to consume the same good. In the case of a pure private good, one person's consumption completely precludes any other from sharing in the good. At the opposite extreme for a pure public good, one's consumption in no way affects another's. For private goods the marginal private value equals the marginal social value, and maximization of one implies maximization of the other. For public goods the marginal social value is the sum of the marginal private values. Individuals considering only their own interests would under-value (underproduce) public goods. Between these extremes are goods with externalities that drive a wedge between the private and social valuations.

The competitive market system underlying the Pareto conditions makes no provision for goods for which there is a divergence between private valuation and social valuation. The system is thereby unable to provide criteria for the provision of public goods or goods with associated externalities. If such goods are deemed desirable by society, then devices must be set up for adequately providing them in ways consistent with efficiency requirements.

References

Arrow, K. J. 1962. "Economic Welfare and the Allocation of Resources for Invention." In National Bureau of Economic Research, *The Rate and Direction of Inventive Activity: Economic and Social Factors*. Princeton: Princeton University Press.

Buchanan, J. 1965. "An Economic Theory of Clubs." *Economica* 32:1–14.

Cicchetti, C. J., and V. K. Smith. 1976. *The Costs of Congestion: An Econometric Analysis of Wilderness*. Cambridge: Ballinger.

Clarke, E. H. 1971. "Multipart Pricing of Public Goods." *Public Choice* 11:17–33.

———. 1972. "Multipart Pricing of Public Goods: An Example." In *Public Prices for Public Products*, ed. S. Mushkin, Washington: Urban Institute.

Groves, T. 1973. "Incentives in Teams." *Econometrica* 41:617–33.

Hurwicz, L. 1972. "On Informationally Decentralised Systems." In *Decision and Organization*, ed. R. Radner and B. McGuire. Amsterdam: North-Holland.

Mohring, H., and H. Mitchell. 1962. *Highway Benefits: An Analytical Framework*. Evanston: Northwestern University Press.

Musgrave, R. A., and P. B. Musgrave. 1973. *Public Finance in Theory and Practice*. New York: McGraw-Hill.

Samuelson, P. A. 1955. "Diagrammatic Exposition of a Theory of Public Expenditure." *The Review of Economics and Statistics* 37:350–56.

Sandler, T., and J. T. Tschirhart. 1980. "The Economic Theory of Clubs: An Evaluative Survey." *Journal of Economic Literature* 18:1481–1521.

Tideman, T. N., and G. Tullock. 1976. "A New and Superior Process for Making Social Choices." *Journal of Political Economy* 84:1145–60.

Tiebout, C. M. 1956. "A Pure Theory of Local Expenditures." *Journal of Political Economy* 64:416–24.

Vickrey, W. 1961. "Counterspeculation, Auctions, and Competitive Sealed Tenders." *Journal of Finance* 16:8–37.

Walters, A. A. 1961. "The Theory and Measurement of Private and Social Cost of Highway Congestion." *Econometrica* 29:676–99.

Supplementary Readings

Davis, O. A., and A. B. Whinston. 1967. "On the Distinction between Public and Private Goods." *American Economic Review* 57:360–73.

Groves, T., and J. Ledyard. 1977. "Optimal Allocation of Public Goods: A Solution to the 'Free Rider Problem.'" *Econometrica* 45:783–809.

Lindahl, E. 1958. "Just Taxation: A Positive Solution." In *Classics in the Theory of Public Finance*, ed. R. A. Musgrave and A. Peacock. London: Macmillan.

Chapter 7

INTERNALIZING EXTERNALITIES

Externalities drive a wedge between the private valuation of costs and benefits and the social valuation. Given such divergencies, the competitive market system will not lead to social efficiency. Utility maximization by individuals and profit maximization by firms will not ensure the socially efficient distribution of output or allocation of resources. In this chapter we examine the nature of this wedge and some of the means available for making private and social values compatible.

Private and Social Costs

In the absence of external effects, the true opportunity cost of production equals the private cost to the firm. Private and social costs are the same. Production that leads to negative externalities implies social costs are greater than private cost, while positive externalities imply the opposite.[1] It will be easier in subsequent discussions if we denote negative externalities as cases where social cost exceeds private cost, and positive externalities where social benefits exceed private benefits.

Social cost exceeds private cost because the producer is able to use as a factor some resource at less than its true opportunity cost. A paint manufacturing firm that expels waste into a nearby stream need not

---

[1] Assume a steel mill and laundry adjoin one another. The social cost of steel production exceeds the private cost if production pollutes the air because the cost to the laundry of cleaning clothes increases (it may be necessary to use dryers rather than hanging clothes out to dry). If, on the other hand, the steel mill lights its plant so well that the laundry is able to cut its electricity bill, the social cost of steel production is less than the private cost. From the electricity costs of the steel mill should be deducted the savings of the laundry.

include waste removal in its cost of production. The use of the stream by the firm, however, precludes its use for other purposes, which imposes a cost on society. The social cost of paint production includes not only the costs incurred by the firm but also the opportunity cost associated with using the stream for this purpose rather than its most efficient alternative.

Private and Social Benefits

By restricting our discussion to positive external effects, we can say that social benefits exceed private benefits when the effect of consumption or production of a particular good on society exceeds the effect on the actual consumer or producer. The utility or production functions of the members of society are not independent. Inoculation of school-aged children against the mumps has the benefit not only of preventing the disease in the inoculated child but also of preventing its spread to other individuals. When the collective benefit exceeds that to an individual, society may provide the good free of charge or subsidize its provision. The benefit of expenditures on research and development to society may exceed the benefit to the firm undertaking such efforts, and therefore such efforts are often supported, at least in part, by the government.

Since costs can often be viewed as negative benefits and benefits as negative costs, knowing how best to represent externalities is difficult. In subsequent discussions, you might find an alternative approach more suitable than that used here. There is a tendency to confuse production externalities with external economies and diseconomies of scale. The latter arise because of increases in the scale of operations, the former because of interdependencies between production functions. As the scale increases, so does the likelihood of interdependencies, but there is no necessary scale factor associated with externalities.

Distorting Effects of Externalities

Figure 7.1 depicts a market situation characterized by negative externalities. The marginal social cost of production (MSC) is greater than the marginal cost to the firm or the marginal private cost (MPC). Assuming the firm produces a good Y in a competitive product market,

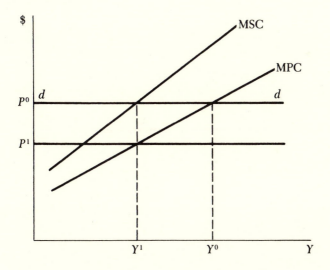

Figure 7.1   Negative Externalities (Production Externalities)

the demand (*dd*) will be infinitely elastic at the market-determined price. The firm acting independently would produce Y^0 units at a price P^0, but the cost to society of Y^0 units is greater than the cost to the firm. The socially optimal output level would be Y^1, where price is equal to the marginal private cost plus the externality, or the marginal social cost. The competitive market system would lead to overproduction of this good.

In Figure 7.2 we depict a situation where the marginal private value of Y (MPV) to a particular consumer is less than the value to society (MSV). Assuming, as in a competitive market, the supply of Y is infinitely elastic at P^0, Y^0 units will be consumed. The value to society of the marginal unit is in excess of P^0 because of the positive externalities. The social optimum level of consumption would be Y^1 units. As is obvious, positive externalities lead to underconsumption (production) while negative externalities lead to overconsumption (production).

Accounting for Externalities

The means available to account for externalities are not unlike the approaches taken in Chapter 5 to controlling monopolists. Taxes and subsidies act in a way similar to tax and price controls on monopolies.

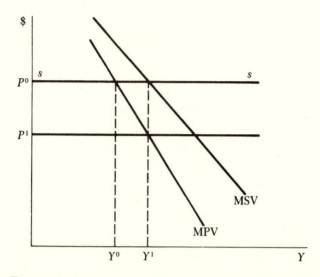

Figure 7.2   Positive Externalities (Consumption Externalities)

Alternatively, the government may directly intervene through regulation, operation, or ownership. In our earlier discussion we viewed these as increasing forms of government intervention. This time we will begin with taxes and subsidies since limitations of this approach have been responsible, in part, for the growing interest in *property rights*.

Taxes and Subsidies

A. C. Pigou (1932) is primarily responsible for developing the notion of an externality as a divergence between private and social costs and benefits. We will focus here on his discussion of negative externalities and their likely effects on society. Smoke pollution from a factory or sparks from a railway train capable of igniting the surrounding forest are two examples. The solution required imposition of a tax on the firm equal to the difference between the marginal private and marginal social cost ($P^0 - P^1$). With reference to Figure 7.1, a tax would be imposed so that at Y^1 units, the marginal private cost plus the tax is just equal to the marginal social cost.

Analogously, to stimulate consumption of goods with positive externalities, subsidies could be imposed. To achieve the socially optimal level of consumption in Figure 7.2, a subsidy equal to the difference between P^0 and P^1 would be needed. A simple example will help to illustrate both the attributes and limitations of such an approach.

An Example of "Taxing the Polluter"

Consider a firm producing steel (Y_1) with a single-variable factor labor (X_1). Rather than state the production function in terms of output, we will express it as labor required for any level of output, or:

$$X_1 = X_1(Y_1). \tag{7.1}$$

The first-order partial can be interpreted as the marginal cost in labor equivalents of Y_1. This value is assumed to be positive as is the second-order partial.

A neighboring laundry produces Y_2 using labor X_2 but is adversely affected by the steel production because of the smoke pollution generated. This will be captured by stating the labor requirements function of Y_2 as:

$$X_2 = X_2(Y_2, Y_1). \tag{7.2}$$

The partial derivative of X_2 with respect to Y_1 is positive. Additional steel production will increase the labor input into the laundry to compensate for the pollution that makes it more difficult to clean clothes.

Total resources in the economy $(\overline{X})$ consist of labor used in producing X_1, X_2 and labor time consumed as leisure (X_3). Social utility (U) is a function of goods produced and leisure. The objective function and first-order maximizing conditions are as follows:

$$\max W = U(Y_1, Y_2, X_3) + \lambda[\overline{X} - X_1(Y_1) - X_2(Y_2, Y_1) - X_3], \tag{7.3}$$

$$\frac{\partial W}{\partial Y_1} = \frac{\partial U}{\partial Y_1} - \lambda\left[\frac{\partial X_1}{\partial Y_1} + \frac{\partial X_2}{\partial Y_1}\right] = 0, \tag{7.4}$$

$$\frac{\partial W}{\partial Y_2} = \frac{\partial U}{\partial Y_2} - \lambda\frac{\partial X_2}{\partial Y_2} = 0, \tag{7.5}$$

$$\frac{\partial W}{\partial X_3} = \frac{\partial U}{\partial X_3} - \lambda = 0. \tag{7.6}$$

$$\frac{\partial W}{\partial \lambda} = [\overline{X} - X_1(Y_1) - X_2(Y_2, Y_1) - X_3] = 0.$$

The term in brackets in (7.4) may be thought of as the marginal social cost of steel production. It includes the direct labor required and the indirect labor to maintain laundry output in the face of pollution. The latter would constitute the externality measured in labor equivalents. Optimality requires that the rate of commodity substitution between steel and the laundry equals the ratio of the marginal social cost of steel to the marginal cost of the laundry.

This approach to the problem has some serious reservations. First, it is formulated with a bias against the steel producer since it requires that one party be held responsible. Second, it is very difficult to measure accurately the damage done. Can we precisely measure the additional labor required by the laundry and then value it at some wage? R. Coase (1960) has shown that a viable system of property rights can provide a more efficient device for addressing the issues of culpability and measurability associated with externalities.

Property Rights

In our previous example the steel mill was held responsible, but if the laundry had been located farther away from the mill, it could have avoided the effects of the pollution. Is the laundry at fault then for locating too close to the mill? Does it matter who located first? Externalities involve reciprocity: the steel mill gives off pollution, but the laundry must be in a position to receive it.

Possibly much of the laundry's business comes from employees of the mill. If we tax the mill, production could be cut, employment reduced, and the laundry's revenue possibly reduced. The loss in revenue may be greater than the cost of pollution. There are, in other words, countless direct and indirect effects that must be considered in measuring the true opportunity cost of pollution. Obviously, in multisector economies these difficulties become greater and more immeasurable.

Assuming a market with *costless transactions,* Coase poses the problem in this way: How much would the laundry be willing to pay the steel mill to eliminate the smoke? Alternatively, How much would the mill be willing to compensate the laundry for the right to emit the smoke? Whether the mill should compensate the laundry for damages, or whether the laundry should bribe the mill into not polluting depends on who owns or has property rights to the environment. These questions may have a familiar ring. They are very similar to the Hicks, Kaldor compensation tests of an earlier chapter.

The thrust of Coase's argument, often referred to as "Coase's Theorem," is that with costless market transactions the initial delimitation of property rights, provided they exist, does not matter in efficiency terms. Property rights internalize the externalities ensuring excludability. Efficiency can be realized by establishing a contractual system that will permit the market mechanism to determine the social value of pollution. It doesn't matter whether the mill, the laundry, or some third party is given initial ownership of the environment or the right to pollute. The government might establish a voucher system in which firms could purchase the right to emit certain levels of pollutants. The mill could buy rights from the government, while the laundry could buy rights from the mill or from the government to prevent their use by the mill.

Direct Intervention

Where transactions are not costless because of legal prohibitions or injunctions against transfer, the initial vesting of property rights will affect realization of efficiency. Where permissible, realignment will occur only when the gain is greater than the cost of the rearrangement, but many of the resultant agreements among producers are likely to be viewed as collusive and thereby illegal according to our earlier-discussed antitrust legislation.

Transaction costs tend to increase as the number of parties involved grows. The environment is the property of all members of society, and the problems involved in petitioning ownership and establishing an efficient market mechanism are so great as to preclude its feasibility. In this and similar situations, the government may assume the role of protector of the communal interest by legislating control of the externality. It may impose restrictions on the level and kinds of pollutants that firms may emit.

When none of the procedures thus far mentioned are effective, the government or some group vested by the government may assume direct control or operation of the affected sectors. This is the situation in oil fields where oil pumping at one well decreases the gas pressure necessary for pumping at other wells. As a consequence, separate firms have an incentive to overpump and overdrill, thereby reducing the oil outtake of competitors. To prevent this situation, firms are given shares in the overall operation of the oil field in exchange for ownership rights in their wells. Their profitability then becomes a function of the amount of oil pumped by the field rather than by a particular well. While one might think that such agreements would evolve voluntarily, it has been necessary to legislate that all oil companies in a field participate. Should one company choose not to comply, it would be at the expense of those that do. Particularly, in the case of positive externalities and when the external effects tend to be very large relative to the private effects, direct government provision (Food and Drug Administration, National Institute for Mental Health, etc.) or government funding may be necessary. We will conclude this chapter with an example.

Research and Development Expenditures–Positive Externalities

Although we will limit our discussion to two firms, the treatment can easily be generalized.[2] Each firm is assumed to produce a single output (Y_1 and Y_2, respectively). The production functions may be represented as:

$$Y_i = A_i f_i(X_i), \qquad i = 1,2, \tag{7.7}$$

where X_i is the labor input and A_i an invention possibilities function. Capital is excluded by assuming it to be invariant or measurable in labor unit equivalents. Technological change is assumed to enter in a Hicksian "neutral" sense or multiplicatively. The invention possibilities function is determined by the firm's own investment in research and development (R_i) and by the technological change of the other firm that it can absorb at zero cost:

$$A_i = a_i(R_i) + \lambda_{ji} a_j(R_j), \qquad i = 1,2; \qquad 0 < \lambda'_{ji} < 1. \tag{7.8}$$

The term λ_{ji} is the proportion of the technology of firm j that can be diffused and absorbed by firm i at zero cost. It is a measure of the "spillover" from j to i. Given a wage of labor r, the price of a research input s, and product price P_i, and assuming profit maximization by the firm and constant prices, the objective function and first-order conditions will be:

$$\max \pi_i = P_i[a_i(R_i) + \lambda_{ji} a_j(R_j)] f_i(X_i) - rX_i - sR_i, \qquad i,j = 1,2, \tag{7.9}$$

$$\frac{\partial \pi_i}{\partial R_i} = P_i \frac{\partial a_i(R_i)}{\partial R_i} f_i(X_i) - s = 0, \tag{7.10}$$

---

[2] Much of this section is taken from an earlier article by this author: "A Comparative Static Model for the Pareto Optimal Allocation of Expenditures on Research and Development," *American Economist* 22:20–21.

$$\frac{\partial \pi_i}{\partial X_i} = P_i[a_i(R_i) + \lambda_{ji}\, a_j(R_j)]\frac{\partial f_i}{\partial X_i} - r = 0. \qquad (7.11)$$

From (7.10) it is obvious that each firm acting independently fails to consider the effects of its research input on other sectors of the economy. Each firm will hire research inputs up to the point where the marginal value product (MVP) (marginal physical product times product price) is just equal to its price (s). The ratio of the private marginal physical product of research to that of labor will equal the ratio of their factor prices.

We will now view the problem from the social perspective of maximizing output subject to a market-clearing constraint that total revenue should equal total cost. Denoting the Lagrangian as δ, the objective function and first-order conditions will be:

$$\max W = [a_1(R_1) + \lambda_{21}a_2(R_2)]f_1(X_1) + [a_2(R_2) + \lambda_{12}a_1(R_1)]f_2(X_2)$$

$$+ \delta[P_1Y_1 + P_2Y_2 - r(X_1 + X_2) - s(R_1 + R_2)] \qquad i,j = 1,2. \quad (7.12)$$

$$\frac{\partial W}{\partial R_i} = \frac{\partial a_i(R_i)}{\partial R_i}\, f_i(X_i) + \lambda_{ij}\frac{\partial a_i(R_i)}{\partial R_i}\, f_j(X_j) - \delta s = 0, \qquad (7.13)$$

$$\frac{\partial W}{\partial X_i} = [a_i(R_i) + \lambda_{ji}a_j(R_j)]\frac{\partial f_i(X_i)}{\partial X_i} - \delta r = 0, \qquad (7.14)$$

$$\frac{\partial W}{\partial \delta} = \sum_{i=1}^{2}[P_iY_i - rX_i - sR_i] = 0. \qquad (7.15)$$

From (7.10) the marginal physical product of research to the firm undertaking the research is:

$$\frac{\partial a_i(R_i)}{\partial R_i}\, f_i(X_i).$$

From (7.13) the marginal social product is R_i is:

$$\frac{\partial a_i(R_i)}{\partial R_i}f_i(X_i) + \lambda_{ij}\frac{\partial a_i(R_i)}{\partial R_i}\, f_j(X_j).$$

The externality of research and development of firm i is:

$$\lambda_{ij}\frac{\partial a_i(R_i)}{\partial R_i}f_j(X_j).$$

It is determined by the ability of firm j to absorb the technology of i (λ_{ij}), the marginal productivity of R_i in firm i, the diffusion of this freely acquired knowledge over the labor input of firm j, and the productivity of X_j.

The private and social marginal productivities of research are drawn in Figure 7.3 and labeled respectively MPP and MSP. Under competitive conditions the firm will hire research inputs to the point where their real price (s/P_i) equals their marginal physical product. The social optimal point would require equality between the real price and the marginal social product. The question we must address is what policies are available to ensure a level of research equal to R_i^2 in Figure 7.3.

As is frequently the case, the government could subsidize research and development by lowering its real price so that equality of the latter with the firm's marginal physical product schedule occurs at R_i^2. Through patents, copyright laws, and other arrangements, a system of property rights in technological advances could be established. This in effect renders the spillover (λ_{ij}) equal to zero. As indicated earlier, given a system of property rights, efficiency can be realized, assuming an effective market system for these rights and insignificant transaction costs. The greater the externalities and the more extensive the spillover, the larger the "free-rider" problems become and the less likely the private sector will undertake production. It may be necessary, then, for the government to do the research itself (e.g., the Food and

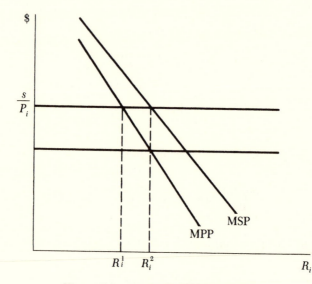

Figure 7.3   Research and Development

Drug Administration researches consumer products), or to fund the research outside the private sector (e.g., research contracts to educational institutions or nonprofit research agencies).

Summary

Controlling and adjusting to externalities is a very difficult problem. The role of the government ranges from that of an overseer ensuring a competitive environment to one of direct ownership and production. Each problem has its own unique properties, and generalization is difficult. The classic illustration of externalities, in which bees obtain nectar from a nearby apple orchard and in return pollinate the orchard, thus increasing the harvest, clearly illustrates the reciprocal nature of most externalities. Should the beekeeper compensate the orchard owner or vice versa?

References

Arrow, K. J. 1962. "Economic Welfare and the Allocation of Resources for Invention." In National Bureau of Economic Research, *The Rate and Direction of Inventive Activity: Economic and Social Factors.* Princeton: Princeton University Press.

Coase, R. H. 1960. "The Problem of Social Cost." *Journal of Law and Economics* 3:1–44.

O'Connell, J. F. 1978. "A Comparative Static Model for the Pareto Optimal Allocation of Expenditures on Research and Development." *American Economist* 22:20–21.

Pigou, A. C. 1932. *The Economics of Welfare,* 4th ed. London: Macmillan.

Supplementary Readings

Bailey, M. N. 1972. "Research and Development Costs and Returns: The U.S. Pharmaceutical Industry." *Journal of Political Economy* 80:70–85.

Bell, F. W. 1972. "Technological Externalities and Common-Property Resources: An Empirical Study of the U.S. Northern Lobster Fishery." *Journal of Political Economy* 80:148–58.

Shapley, L. S., and M. Shubik. 1969. "On the Case of an Economic System with Externalities." *American Economic Review* 59:678–87.

Starrett, D. 1973. "A Note on Externalities and the Core." *Econometrica* 41:179–83.

Wheaton, W. C. 1972. "On the Possibility of a Market for Externalities." *Journal of Political Economy* 80:1029–44.

Chapter 8

DYNAMIC OPTIMIZATION: THE PROBLEM OF CONTROL

Until now our analysis has focused on the conditions necessary to ensure a maximizing state. The discussion was a comparative static, with time entering in only an implicit or definitional way. We implicitly assumed the necessary maximizing conditions could be achieved instantaneously, so we did not have to consider an explicit adjustment process. Variables were defined with reference to time as being measured over an interval (flow variables) or at a particular point (stock variables). At the very least we have been myopic, and possibly simplistic, since there is really little sense in treating the properties of an equilibrium unless some dynamic process ensures at least the possibility of reaching the equilibrium.

Conceptually, the question of dynamics (whether there exists a mechanism moving the system to a particular position) precedes comparative statics (properties of the system at the position). Pedagogically, there seem to be advantages by beginning our discussion at a moment in time, assuming such a state exists, and then gradually extending the time frame. You may find the above a rather esoteric rationale for the order of topics discussed. More pragmatically, the question of optimizing a system over time is more difficult than optimizing at a point in time, and knowing the comparative static conditions will make the discussion of dynamics somewhat easier.

Methodology

A number of mathematical techniques have developed over the last century to solve problems of optimizing over time. Although we will consider an approach known as *control theory*, the calculus of variations and dynamic programming have been used in both economic and noneconomic problems. Our choice of approach is based on two factors. First, control theory, or the "maximum principle," tends to be used most in economics. Second, this methodology bears considerable resemblance to the Lagrangian multiplier technique discussed earlier.

In the twentieth century the adoption of a particular expositional approach in economics appears to be a lagged response to methodological developments in mathematics and the natural sciences. The *marginalism* of A. Marshall's *Principles of Economics*, 9th ed. (1920) used the burgeoning areas of differential and integral calculus. The set theory approach to general equilibrium reflects the advances in real and abstract analysis. Some would even argue that attention to questions of general equilibrium reflects earlier biological studies of the human circulatory system. Recent developments in *catastrophe theory* by the noted mathematician René Thom have already seen applications by Zeeman (1976) to the stock market crash, and more will certainly follow.

Development of the space program necessitated mathematical advances in the areas of dynamic programming, the calculus of variations, and the maximum principle. These advances have now been taken up by economists. In the same way that such terms as the "margin" and the "core" have become mainstays in the economist's lexicon, so this new dynamic approach has its own terminology. A control problem consists of the following components: time, state variables, equations of motion, and an objective functional. Those with a strong background in mathematics are referred to Pontryagin *et al.* (1962). Our approach will be considerably more heuristic and intuitive. We will begin our discussion with the dynamic conditions for Pareto optimality and then move on to a discussion of control theory.

Pareto Optimality Over Time

In the same way that we derived the conditions for efficiency at a point in time by examining the behavior of individual economic agents, we can now ask how consumers and firms should act to maximize over time. As in our earlier discussion, we will assume a purely competitive economy. Throughout attention will be paid to the similarities and differences between the comparative static and dynamic optimizing conditions.

Consumer Behavior

To simplify the analysis somewhat, we will assume a two-period time horizon on the part of the consumer. Consumption today will be denoted C_1 and consumption tomorrow, C_2. Utility is now a function of C_1 and C_2, and assuming the utility function satisfies the same properties it did earlier, one could derive a series of indifference curves between present and future consumption similar to those derived earlier for different goods at a single point in time. The negative of the slope of the indifference curves represents the trade-off between present and future consumption, which will be referred to as the "marginal rate of time preference" (MTP):

$$\text{MTP} = \frac{-\Delta C_2}{\Delta C_1}.$$

As expected, the amount of future consumption one is willing to sacrifice for current consumption declines as the latter increases. The location of the indifference curves will give some insight into the personalities of the individuals we are dealing with. Impatient, risk-adverse, myopic individuals will have indifference curves lying close to the axis measuring C_1, indicating a predisposition for current consumption. The more farsighted, risk prone, patient types will have indifference maps closer to the C_2 axis, indicating an inclination toward future consumption.

We will denote income in period one as M_1 and that in two as M_2. If there were no consumption in period one, the amount available for future consumption, what we will call wealth in two (W_2) will be:

$$W_2 = M_2 + M_1(1 + i), \tag{8.1}$$

where i is the rate of interest per day earnable on money that is saved. If there were no consumption in two, consumption in one would equal M_1, plus the amount that could be borrowed against income in period two or the present value of M_2. This sum will be referred to as wealth in period one (W_1):

$$W_1 = M_1 + \frac{M_2}{1 + i}. \tag{8.2}$$

In our earlier discussion the slope of the budget constraint was the negative of the price ratio, but now the price of current consumption is not only the price per unit P_1 but also the lost savings by the decision to spend (iP_1) or $P_1(1 + i)$. Assuming future prices do not change ($P_2 = P_1$), the slope of the price line will be $-(1 + i)$. The budget constraint and the point of tangency between it and the indifference map are depicted in Figure 8.1. Intertemporal utility maximization implies equality between the marginal rate of time preference and the discount rate of $(1 + i)$. An increase in the interest rate lowers current wealth (W_1) and increases future wealth (W_2), thus increasing the slope of the budget line. The substitution effect would lead to greater future consumption since current consumption would imply a loss of i. The income effect, on the other hand, depends on whether the consumer is a borrower or lender. If the former, higher-interest rates decrease income while just the opposite occurs for a lender.

In the same way that we earlier found efficiency in exchange for different commodities, we could now find the locus of current and future commodity combinations at which the marginal rates of time preference are equal among consumers. Consumption less than wealth implies savings and lending, while consumption in excess of wealth implies an equal amount of dissaving or borrowing.

Firm Behavior

We will begin with the simplest case in which C_1 and C_2 are viewed as separate goods. Factors in a given time period are fixed and allocated toward production of either in such a way that the rates of technical substitution between factors in the production of C_1 and C_2 are equal.[1] The question of how these resources, some of which may be non-renewable, should be utilized will be deferred to a later section. Figure 8.2 represents the intertemporal production transformation curve for C_1 and C_2. Efficiency in production is ensured along the curve, and its concavity indicates declining returns to intertemporal substitution. The negative of the slope is referred to as the intertemporal rate of product transformation. As was pointed out earlier, however, such

---

[1] The reader may want to refer to the discussion of production in Chapter 2.

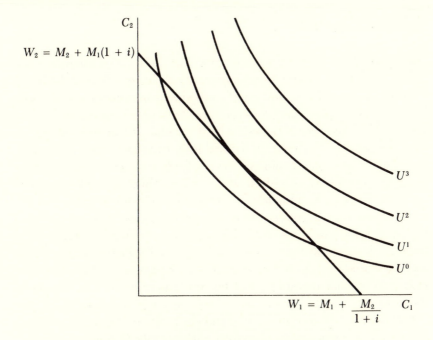

Figure 8.1   Optimizing Consumption Over Time

efficiency is consistent with many different distributions of utility. In contrast to our previous example, though, we must now consider distributions, not only at a point in time but also over time.

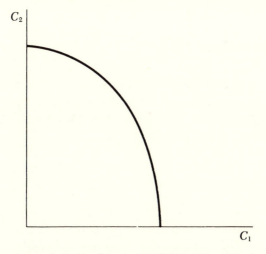

Figure 8.2   Production Possibilities Over Time

Social Discount Rate

Since optimality requires an assessment of the relative importance of present and future generations, some authors have called for the introduction of a *social discount* rate, embodying intergenerational social preferences, in place of the interest rate discussed previously. Solow (1974) gives a number of reasons why the social rate might be set lower than the private rate. First, individual interest rates include a factor for individual risk. At least some of these refer to transfer or distributional changes, which may affect individuals but would cancel out for society as a whole. Second, individuals are concerned with after-tax returns while before-tax returns are more relevant for society. Consideration of after-tax profit would require a higher discount factor. Finally, while individuals may discount the future because of selfishness or myopia, society should not, since future members of society are no less important than current members. Indeed, one might argue that the social discount rate should be zero in a completely egalitarian society.

Optimality between production and consumption would occur when the social rate equaled the intergenerational rate of product transformation. The social discount serves as a convenient tool, but the problems involved in its determination clearly are sufficient to render one cautious in its use. As in the comparative static case, we are ultimately led to consideration of a social welfare function to arrive at a unique optimizing position. In this case, however, both the objective and constraints are functions of time.

Rudiments of Control Theory

In this section we postulate a welfare function and derive the conditions for optimization. As in the discussion of Chapter 3, we assume the existence of the function and defer until later consideration of the issues involved in its formulation.

Objective Functional

Our objective is to maximize welfare W over T time periods. In contrast to the comparative static case, the solution will not be in terms of the levels of certain variables but functions defining the behavior of variables. We will refer to that which is being maximized as the objective functional. Variables that affect welfare but are outside the decision makers' control are referred to as state variables (X), while discretionary variables that can be controlled are denoted V. One may interpret these terms as referring to single variables or vectors; however, we will limit our discussion to the single-variable case. Time (t) is continuously measurable, and, since individuals may have temporal preferences, it enters explicitly into the objective functional. The problem is to maximize the following:

$$W[X(t),V(t),t] = \int_t^T W[X(t),V(t),t]dt. \tag{8.3}$$

Constraints

The state variable X is assumed to change over time. The equation of motion describing its behavior can be defined as

$$\overset{o}{X}(t) = M[X(t),V(t),t]. \tag{8.4}$$

If $X(t)$ is capital, $\overset{o}{X}(t)$ will be investment determined by the size of the capital stock, the value of the instrument variable, and time. Our goal is to maximize (8.3) with respect to V, subject to (8.4) and certain initial conditions regarding the value of the state variable $[X(t) = \overline{X}]$.

Solution

Assume a small time interval Δ. Given the initial values of X and a selection of instruments V over the interval, the value of X at time $t + \Delta$ can be determined by (8.4). Yet the time interval is so short that V does not change but is maintained at $\overline{V}$. We can now rewrite the objective functional as:

$$W[X(t),\overline{V},t]\Delta + \int_{t+\Delta}^T W[X(t + \Delta),V(t),t + \Delta]dt. \tag{8.5}$$

Note carefully the change in time between the two terms in (8.5). In the second term, time begins at $t + \Delta$, and the state variables are evaluated at $t + \Delta$.

Let V^* be the best choice of V from t on, so that

$$V^* [X(t),t] = \max W[X(t),V(t),t]. \tag{8.6}$$

$V*$ does not involve V since the maximizing choice of V is assumed. Let the policy $\overline{V}$ be pursued in period Δ and the maximizing policy from $t + \Delta$ onward. The effect on welfare will then be

$$W[X(t),\overline{V},t]\Delta + V*[X(t + \Delta),t + \Delta]. \qquad (8.7)$$

The problem is now one of finding the value of $\overline{V}$ that will maximize the first term in (8.7), which is called the *intermediate function*, and, having found that, we will maximize W. The second term, called the *final function*, shows the dependence of the objective on the terminal state $X(t + \Delta)$ and terminal time $(t + \Delta)$ of the interval Δ.

The case when there is only one state variable can be illustrated with the help of Figure 8.3. From the alternative feasible projectories encompassed by ABC, our objective is to choose the optimal one determined by our choice of $\overline{V}$. The locus of terminal values of X is denoted by EF. The optimal trajectory resulting in $X(t + \Delta)$ is BD.

Assuming that the partial derivative is zero at the maximum, we can differentiate (8.7) to obtain:

$$\Delta\frac{\partial}{\partial\overline{V}}W[X(t),\overline{V},t] + \frac{\partial}{\partial\overline{V}}V*[X(t + \Delta),t + \Delta] = 0.^2 \qquad (8.8)$$

The second term in (8.8) requires we know $V*$; in addition, $\overline{V}$ enters not directly but only via its effect on $X(t + \Delta)$. Rewriting, we obtain:

$$\frac{\partial V*}{\partial\overline{V}} = \frac{\partial V*}{\partial X(t + \Delta)} \cdot \frac{\partial X(t + \Delta)}{\partial\overline{V}}. \qquad (8.9)$$

Over a short time span, $X(t + \Delta)$ can be approximated by $X(t) + \overset{o}{X}(t)\Delta$, where the new level of X is equal to the original level plus its rate of change $\overset{o}{X}(t)$ times the time interval Δ. Since $\overset{o}{X}(t)$ has already been defined, we can write:

$$X(t + \Delta) = X(t) + \overset{o}{X}(t)\Delta,$$

where

$$\overset{o}{X}(t) = M[X(t),V(t),t]$$

---

[2] The derivative may not vanish at the maximum, and it may also equal zero at a minimum. For the time being we will ignore these possibilities. The analysis that follows draws heavily on that of Dorfman (1969).

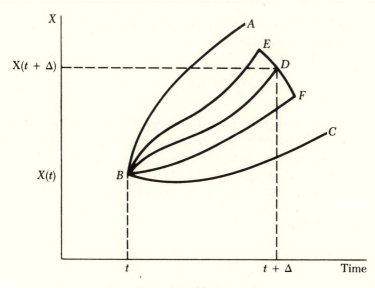

Figure 8.3   Feasible Trajectories

and

$$\frac{\partial X(t + \Delta)}{\partial \overline{V}} = \Delta \frac{\partial M}{\partial \overline{\overline{V}}}.$$

The first term on the right in (8.9) measures the effect of a change in the state variable in time $t + \Delta$ on the maximum possible utility from $t + \Delta$ on. It is the marginal value of X at time $t + \Delta$. We will denote the marginal value of the state variable at time t by $\lambda(t)$, so that:

$$\lambda(t) = \frac{\partial V^*}{\partial X(t)}.$$

Substituting these results into (8.8) yields:

$$\frac{\partial W}{\partial \overline{\overline{V}}} + \lambda(t + \Delta)\Delta \frac{\partial M}{\partial \overline{V}} = 0. \tag{8.10}$$

Further, we can approximate $\lambda(t + \Delta)$ by $\lambda(t)$, plus the rate of change in λ over time $(\overset{o}{\lambda}(t))$, times the interval Δ. Inserting this into (8.10) yields:

$$\frac{\partial W}{\partial \overline{\overline{V}}} + \lambda(t)\frac{\partial M}{\partial \overline{V}} + \overset{o}{\lambda}(t)\Delta \frac{\partial M}{\partial \overline{\overline{V}}} = 0. \tag{8.11}$$

As Δ approaches zero, we can disregard the last term, and a necessary major optimality condition becomes:

$$\frac{\partial W}{\partial \overline{V}} + \lambda(t)\frac{\partial M}{\partial \overline{V}} = 0. \tag{8.12}$$

The above has a straightforward economic interpretation. At every instant in time V should be chosen so that its marginal immediate effect on welfare is just equal to the marginal value of X times its long-run effect on the accumulation of X. The latter term $-\lambda(t)\partial M/\partial \overline{V}$ may be interpreted as the marginal cost measured in terms of X.

Assuming $\overline{V}$ is chosen to satisfy (8.12), our objective functional will be maximized. Thus:

$$V^*[X(t),t] = W[X(t),\overline{V},t]\Delta + V^*[X(t + \Delta),t + \Delta]. \tag{8.13}$$

Differentiating with respect to X yields $\lambda(t)$ on the left; proceeding as previously and rewriting, one gets:

$$-\overset{o}{\lambda}(t) = \frac{\partial W}{\partial X} + \lambda(t)\frac{\partial M}{\partial X}.^3 \tag{8.14}$$

This represents another major formula and is also subject to an economic interpretation. The term $\overset{o}{\lambda}$ is the rate of change in the value of X. The negative of $\overset{o}{\lambda}$ is then the depreciation rate of X. Maximization requires that the loss in the value of X should equal the contribution X makes to welfare $(\partial W/\partial X)$, plus the contribution X makes to the value of X at the end of the interval $[\lambda(t)\partial M/\partial X]$.

Equations (8.4), (8.12), and (8.14) stated below represent the *maximum principle* of control theory:

---

[3] The intervening steps are as follows:

$$\lambda(t) = \Delta\frac{\partial W}{\partial X} + \frac{\partial}{\partial X} V^*[X(t + \Delta),t + \Delta],$$

$$= \Delta\frac{\partial W}{\partial X} + \frac{\partial X(t + \Delta)}{\partial X}\lambda(t + \Delta),$$

$$= \Delta\frac{\partial W}{\partial X} + \left(1 + \Delta\frac{\partial M}{\partial X}\right)(\lambda + \overset{o}{\lambda}\Delta),$$

$$= \Delta\frac{\partial W}{\partial X} + \lambda + \Delta\lambda\frac{\partial M}{\partial X} + \Delta\overset{o}{\lambda} + \overset{o}{\lambda}\frac{\partial M}{\partial X}\Delta^2.$$

Assuming Δ^2 is sufficiently small to ignore, canceling and rearranging yields (8.14).

$$\overset{o}{X}(t) = M[X(t),V(t),t],\tag{8.4}$$

$$\frac{\partial W}{\partial \overline{V}} + \lambda(t)\frac{\partial M}{\partial \overline{V}} = 0,\tag{8.12}$$

$$-\overset{o}{\lambda}(t) = \frac{\partial W}{\partial X} + \lambda(t)\frac{\partial M}{\partial X}.\tag{8.14}$$

Realization of these conditions ensures that the objective functional (8.3) repeated below will be maximized.

$$W[X(t),V(t),t] = \int_{0}^{T} W[X(t),V(t),t]dt.\tag{8.3}$$

Alternative Derivation

An alternative approach, which bears a close resemblance to the technique of Lagrange, involves the formulation of an auxiliary or *Hamiltonian function*:

$$H = W(X,V,t) + \lambda(t)M(X,V,t).\tag{8.15}$$

The term $\lambda(t)$ may be thought of as the dynamic equivalent of the Lagrangian multiplier and is called a *costate variable*.[4] The maximum principle stated in terms of the Hamiltonian is then:

$$\frac{\partial H}{\partial \lambda} = \overset{o}{X},\tag{8.4$'$}$$

$$\frac{\partial H}{\partial V} = 0,\tag{8.12$'$}$$

$$\frac{\partial H}{\partial X} = -\overset{o}{\lambda}.\tag{8.14$'$}$$

The equation numbers correspond to the analogous conditions derived earlier.

---

[4] The Hamiltonian is defined as the sum of the intermediate function of the objective functional plus the inner product of the costate variables and the functions defining the rate of change of the state variables.

Boundary Conditions

Thus far we have avoided the question of what the initial state of the economy is or the possibility of prescribing specific terminal values. These issues constitute the *boundary conditions* of our problem. Numerous specifications of boundary conditions are possible, and each in turn poses specific problems. For example, if the objective is to maximize welfare from time t to T, then the marginal value of X in T, $\lambda(T)$, should equal zero, but if a bequest is desired, it would be positive. If we assume initial values for X but no terminal value, then $\lambda(0)$ must be determined. If a terminal value $X(T) \geqslant \overline{X}$ is included, then our maximizing process must be subject to this condition.

Generalization and Extension: Theorem

We have assumed thus far that maximization occurred when the first order partials vanished in equation (8.8). This is neither a necessary or sufficient condition, and we can state the maximum principle more formally in terms of the following theorem:

THEOREM: *Given an objective function*

$$\int_0^T W[X(t),V(t),t]dt,$$

where $\overset{o}{X}(t) = M[X(t),V(t),t]$, $X(0)$ *is preassigned, and* $X(T) \geqslant \overline{X}$. Both W and M are twice continuously differentiable with respect to X, differentiable with respect to V, and continuous with respect to t. Then if $V^*(t)$ is a solution, there exists an auxiliary variable $\lambda(t)$ such that:

1. For each t, $V^*(t)$ maximizes $H[X(t), V(t), \lambda(t),t]$, where H is the Hamiltonian;
2. $\lambda(t)$ satisfies $(d\lambda/dt) = (-\partial H/\partial X)$, evaluated at $X = X(t)$, $V = V^*(t)$, $\lambda = \lambda(t)$; and
3. $X(T) \geqslant \overline{X}$, $\lambda(T) \geqslant 0$, $\lambda(t)[X(T) - \overline{X}] = 0$ (transversality condition).

Condition (3) arises because of the assumption that the terminal value of X should be greater than some minimum. The transversality condition asserts that the terminal value of λ cannot be negative, and that it will be zero if $X(T) > \overline{X}$.

While this discussion has been very superficial, and we have deliberately avoided many of the complexities and difficulties involved, it does provide insight into the nature of the problem. In the next section we will try to reinforce our understanding of maximum principles with an example.

Optimal Capital Accumulation

Consider a very simple economy in which the government controls all productive activity. The economic policy makers are confronted with the problem of allocating resources between consumption and investment so as to maximize consumption per capita over a particular time span. Population (X_2) is assumed to grow exponentially at a rate π:

$$X_2(t) = X_2(0)e^{\pi t}, \tag{8.15}$$

where for convenience it will be assumed that $X_2(0)$ is equal to 1. Consumption per capita is c, while $U(c)$ is the utility derived per person from c. Total utility will be defined very simply as:

$$W = e^{\pi t}U(c). \tag{8.16}$$

If the time rate of social preference is p, the present value (value at time 0) of consumption in time t is:

$$e^{(\pi-p)t}U(c).^5 \tag{8.17}$$

The function to be maximized will then be:

$$W = \int_0^T e^{(\pi-p)t}U(c)dt, \tag{8.18}$$

where T is the time span that could be infinite.

Disregarding technological change and assuming a production function homogeneous of the first degree in capital (X_1) and labor (X_2), output can be expressed as:

$$Y(t) = X_2(t)f[x_1(t)],^6 \tag{8.19}$$

---

[5] We alluded to the problems involved in arriving at a social discount rate earlier. One could substitute a composite interest rate in its place, thus avoiding the problems associated with a social choice mechanism.

[6] Labor and population are assumed synonymous. Our conclusion would not be altered significantly if we introduced a labor force participation rate.

where Y is output and x_1 is the capital/labor ratio. Gross investment will equal output Y minus total consumption $X_2 c$. Assume capital depreciates at a rate δ so that total extinction of X_1 is δX_1. Net capital formation will then be:

$$\overset{o}{X}_1 = Y - X_2 c - \delta X_1 = X_2[f(x_1) - c] - \delta X_2 x_1 = X_2[f(x_1) - c - \delta x_1].$$
(8.20)

The equation of motion for x_1 is:

$$\overset{o}{x}_1 = \frac{dX_1/X_2}{dt} = \frac{X_1}{X_2}\left(\frac{\overset{o}{X}_1}{X_1} - \frac{\overset{o}{X}_2}{X_2}\right) = x_1\left(\frac{\overset{o}{X}_1}{X_2 x_1} - \pi\right).$$
(8.21)

Substituting (8.20) into (8.21) and finding $\overset{o}{x}_1$ yields:

$$\overset{o}{x}_1 = f(x_1) - c - (\pi + \delta)x_1.$$
(8.22)

Equation (8.18) represents the objective functional and (8.22) the equation of motion, which corresponds to (8.4) in our earlier discussion. To derive (8.12), differentiate (8.17) and (8.22) with respect to the choice variable, c:

$$\frac{\partial e^{(\pi-p)t}U(c)}{\partial c} = e^{(\pi-p)t}U'(c),$$
(8.23)

$$\frac{\partial}{\partial c}[f(x_1) - c - (\pi - \delta)x_1] = -1.$$
(8.24)

The second condition is then:

$$e^{(\pi-p)t}U'(c) - \lambda = 0.$$
(8.25)

Where λ was previously the marginal value of a state variable, in this case it is the value of a unit of capital. Condition 2 requires that it equal the marginal utility of consumption adjusted for population growth and the rate of time preference.

The third condition can be derived by differentiating (8.17) and (8.22) with respect to x_1 (where the prime indicates a first-order derivative). The derivative of (8.17) is zero, so we have:

$$-\overset{o}{\lambda} = \lambda[f'(x_1) - (\pi + \delta)], \text{ or}$$

$$f'(x_1) = \pi + \delta - \frac{\overset{o}{\lambda}}{\lambda}. \tag{8.26}$$

The λ term can be eliminated by differentiating (8.25) with respect to time, yielding (where a double prime indicates a second-order derivative):

$$\frac{\overset{o}{\lambda}}{\lambda} = \pi - p + \frac{U''(c)}{U'(c)} \frac{dc}{dt}.^7 \tag{8.27}$$

Equation (8.26) then becomes:

$$f'(x_1) = p + \delta + \frac{U''(c)}{U'(c)} \frac{dc}{dt}, \tag{8.28}$$

which constitutes the final condition for the maximum principle analogous to (8.14). It asserts that along the optimal consumption trajectory the marginal productivity of capital should equal the sum of the rate of time preference p, the depreciation rate δ, and the proportionate rate at which the psychic cost of savings declines over time.

A word is in order about the last term in (8.28). The marginal utility of consumption is $U'(c)$; expressed negatively it is the marginal cost of savings. Its time rate of change is $U''(c)\,dc/dt$, and the resultant ratio is the proportionate rate.

From (8.22) we found the optimal path for x_1:

$$\overset{o}{x}_1 = f(x_1) - c - (\pi + \delta)x_1. \tag{8.22}$$

From (8.28) the path for consumption is:

$$\overset{o}{c} = \frac{U'(c)}{U''(c)} [p + \delta - f'(x_1)]. \tag{8.28}$$

---

[7] Using the product rule and differentiating with respect to time yields:

$$e^{(\pi-p)t} \frac{dU'(c)}{d(c)} \frac{dc}{dt} + U'(c)(\pi - p)e^{(\pi-p)t} - \frac{d\lambda}{dt} = 0.$$

Since

$$\lambda = e^{(\pi-p)t} U'(c),$$

dividing by λ and rewriting, the derivative can be expressed as (8.27).

It is clear that $\overset{o}{x}_1$ will be zero when

$$c = f(x_1) - (\pi - \delta)x_1.$$

Figure 8.4 will make these points clearer. The curve for $\overset{o}{x}_1 = 0$ is drawn to reflect the assumption of positive but diminishing marginal productivity of capital until $\overset{o}{c} = 0$ $[f'(x_1) > 0, f''(x_1) < 0]$. At low levels of capital it is assumed $f'(x_1) > \pi + \delta$, $f(0) = 0$. If c (consumption per capita) is less (greater) than that indicated on the curve $\overset{o}{x}_1 = 0$, capital per capita will expand (decline).

Consumption per capita will not change ($\overset{o}{c} = 0$) if from (8.22):

$$f'(x_1) = p + \delta.$$

To the left of the vertical line $\overset{o}{c} = 0$ in Figure 8.4, consumption per capita will grow. Smaller levels of capital permit more consumption. Once the initial capital to labor ratio is determined, the entire course of the economy can be mapped out. The arrows trace out alternative paths for the system. Beginning at A leads to initial increases in both x_1 and c until the $\overset{o}{c} = 0$ locus is reached, after which c declines. As can be seen, all the trajectories, with the exception of that from A, lead to situations where either c or x_1 is negative. Since this is impossible, the only feasible path is that from A. It leads to a steady state, an equilibrium position, in which neither per capita consumption nor capital

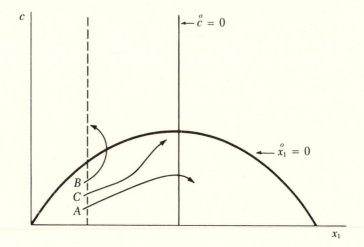

Figure 8.4   Optimal Capital Accumulation

change, which in turn implies that both capital and labor grow at a rate equal to the population growth rate (π). The appropriate path of the system depends crucially on the initial position and the terminal date. If the economy is very close to the optimal path, the best strategy might be to move directly to it. On the other hand, if society is quite far away so that great sacrifice in the form of reduced consumption for current generations would result, then a more gradual move may be in order. The term *turnpike theorem* refers to the treatment of optimal trajectories in moving the system to its dynamic equilibrium.

Dynamic Second-Best Policies

Conditions may arise in which the number of control variables is insufficient to achieve the optimal policy. Analogous to the comparative static case, there may be constraints on the economic system preventing complete optimization. The question then is what is the best policy given the limited number of control variables. The maximum principle can be used to find the second-best policy, but, as you would expect, the problem becomes a great deal more complicated.

Summary

Because the dynamic conditions for efficiency and optimality are so much more complex, they are often ignored in favor of a comparative static analysis. This oversight does not lessen their importance, however; nor does it lessen the intimate interdependencies between statics and dynamics. As will be seen later, in cases such as natural resources there is little alternative to a dynamic treatment. The optimizing criteria with the explicit inclusion of time have analogs in the comparative static conditions, but with a principal difference that the requirements are now functions of time.

This concludes our discussion of the conditions for economic efficiency. In the next several chapters we will concentrate on the issues involved in achieving equity in the distribution of society's product.

References

Dorfman, R. 1969. "An Economic Interpretation of Optimal Control Theory." *The American Economic Review* 59:817–31.

Marshall, A. 1920. *Principles of Economics*, 8th ed. London: Macmillan.

Pontryagin, L. S., V. G. Boltyonskii, R. V. Gamkrelidge, and E. F. Mischenko. 1962. *The Mathematic Theory of Optimal Processes*, trans. K. N. Truogoff. New York: Interscience Publishers.

Solow, R. M. 1974. "The Economics of Resources or the Resources of Economics." *American Economic Review* 64:1–14.

Zeeman, E. C. 1976. "Castastrophe Theory." *Scientific American* 234:65–83.

Supplementary Readings

Arrow, K. J., and M. Kurz. 1970. *Public Investment, the Rate of Return, and Optimal Fiscal Policy*. Baltimore: The Johns Hopkins Press.

Hirshleifer, J. 1980. *Price Theory and Applications*, 2nd ed. Englewood Cliffs, N.J.: Prentice-Hall.

Intriligator, M. D. 1971. *Mathematical Optimization and Economic Theory*. Englewood Cliffs, N.J.: Prentice-Hall.

Mishan, C. J. 1981. *Introduction to Normative Economics*. New York: Oxford University Press.

Quirk, J. P. 1976. *Intermediate Microeconomics*. Chicago: S.R.A.

Roberts, B., and D. L. Schulze. 1973. *Modern Mathematics and Economic Analysis*. New York: W. W. Norton.

Singer, N. M. 1972. *Public Microeconomics*. Boston: Little, Brown.

Chapter 9

IMPLICATIONS FOR THE DISTRIBUTION OF INCOME

Our discussion until now has focused on the product market and the conditions for the realization of policy goals in both a comparative static and dynamic framework. In this chapter we analyze the effects of the market system on the distribution of income. The next chapters will consider methods of altering a given distribution and policies to achieve a more equitable distribution.

Historically in neoclassic microeconomic theory, questions of efficiency have received more attention than concerns for equity. In a capitalist system policies designed to alter income directly are often viewed as socialistic and damaging to the "free enterprise" system. Efficiency is much easier to support since it implies increases in welfare without any trade-off among members of society. In evaluating income distribution policies, a social welfare function that weighs the importance of various societal members is required. This may account for the greater emphasis on distribution in more interventionist socialist governments. Questions of equity are much more predominant in the writing of British and European economists than of the Americans.

In the United States the issue of equity grows in periods of heightened social consciousness. The "New Deal" and "New Frontier" are examples of two such periods. Secularly, as society becomes more aware of its limitations and fixed resources, the issue of how best to distribute the product of these resources becomes more pressing. Realization of the finite and limited quantity of resources may well be responsible for Ricardo (1951) proclaiming that no problem in economics was as important as income distribution.

119

Income, Earnings, and Wealth

Allocation of the economic pie can be measured in many different ways. *Income* is a *flow* of returns to human and nonhuman assets and represents a payment over some time interval. *Wealth,* on the other hand, is the dollar value of a *stock* of assets at a moment in time. Usually these assets are nonhuman; however, in some studies the capitalized earnings of individuals are included as wealth. Bronfenbrenner (1971) points out that in societies that allow slavery the market value of slaves is also included in wealth. *Earnings* or labor income includes wages, salaries, and executive compensation, and excludes property income such as interest, rents, and dividends. Since earnings constitute the major part of total family income, and since income can be more easily regulated than wealth, our discussion will concentrate primarily on the return to labor. The return from individuals who own and operate their own businesses is referred to as "proprietor's income," and includes returns to both labor and property. The distribution of income for the United States is summarized in Table 9.1.

Functional Distribution

We begin our discussion by considering the effects of a competitive economy on income distribution. This is sometimes referred to as the functional distribution of income: how it is distributed by function performed in the economy. In the next chapter we will treat the personal distribution: its relative distribution among segments of society. Our analysis will center on labor and its return in the form of employee compensation, loosely referred to as "the wage."

Marginal Productivity Theory of Income Distribution

In our earlier discussion of a competitive economy, firms were assumed to maximize profit given factor prices. The determination of these prices accounts for the distribution of factor income, and it is to this topic we now turn.

Given the firm's objective of profit maximization, it will hire factors until the marginal physical product times the output price, the marginal value product (MVP), is just equal to the factor price. Let P be the

Table 9.1   U.S. Distribution of Personal Income, 1980

	Billions of Dollars		*Percentage of Total*
Labor income		1,596.5	70.1
Wage and salary	1343.6		
Other labor income	252.9		
Proprietors' income		130.6	5.7
Business and professional	107.2		
Farm	23.4		
Property income		342.6	15.1
Rental income of persons	31.9		
Dividends	54.4		
Personal interest income	256.3		
Transfer payments	294.5		
Less personal contributions for social insurance	−87.9	206.6	9.1
		2,276.3	100.0

Source: Department of Commerce, Bureau of Economic Analysis.

product price, Y be output, P_1 and P_2 be the prices of factors X_1 and X_2, and denote the production function as $f(X_1, X_2)$. Profit, π, will then be:

$$\pi = Pf(X_1, X_2) - P_1 X_1 - P_2 X_2. \tag{9.1}$$

Assuming the production function is well behaved (the first-order partials are positive and the second-orders are negative), the first-order maximizing conditions are:

$$\frac{\partial \pi}{\partial X_1} = P \frac{\partial f}{\partial X_1} - P_1 = 0, \tag{9.2}$$

$$\frac{\partial \pi}{\partial X_2} = P \frac{\partial f}{\partial X_2} - P_2 = 0. \tag{9.3}$$

From the first-order conditions the optimal employment levels of X_1 and X_2 can be observed. The demand schedule for a factor tells the level of employment consistent with profit maximization at various factor prices. If factors are independent of each other so that changes in the price of one factor have no effect on the employment levels of others, the monetized marginal productivity schedule (MVP) would be the factor demand schedule. Keep in mind, the marginal productivity schedule assumes all other factors are held constant. If factors are related in production, an increase (decrease) in the price of one will lead to an increase (decrease) in amounts of the other if they are substitutes and a decrease (increase) if they are complements. If other factors change, the marginal productivity schedule is not invariant.[1]

The assumption that factor price is invariant implies the factor supply schedule for any individual firm will be infinitely elastic at the market-determined price. Given the simplest case where there is only one variable input so that the marginal productivity schedule does not shift, the profit-maximizing level of employment of X_1 will be at X_1^0 in Figure 9.1a.

Aggregation Problems

As a first approximation, one could think of deriving the aggregate demand as the horizontal summation of each firm's demand schedule. As factor price falls, more will be employed and aggregate output will expand. While we assumed previously that product price was constant for any firm regardless of the output level, as all firms expand, output product price will decline even in a competitive model. The marginal value productivity schedule will shift toward the origin, implying less additional employment than would occur at a constant product price. The aggregate demand schedule will thus be less elastic than the sum of individual firms' demand schedules.

As discussed by Marshall (1920) and Hicks (1963), the elasticity of factor demand will be determined by the elasticity of substitution,[2] the elasticity of demand for the final product, the elasticity of supply of other inputs, and the proportion of total costs made up of a particular factor's cost.[3] The elasticity of factor demand is important because it tells us what happens to factor income given factor price changes.

---

[1] For a more complete discussion of this issue see Ferguson (1969).

[2] The elasticity of substitution (σ) in the two-variable case measures the percentage change in factor input ratio divided by the percentage change in the factor price ratio.

$$\sigma = \frac{\Delta(X_2/X_1)}{(X_2/X_1)} \div \frac{\Delta(P_1/P_2)}{(P_1/P_2)}.$$

[3] There is some dispute over the influence of this last determinant. For a summary of the issues involved see P.R.G. Layard and A. A. Walters (1978, chap. 9).

Euler's Theorem Revisited

Restricting our discussion to production functions homogeneous of the first degree, output can be expressed as a linear function of each input times its respective marginal productivity, or:

$$Y = \frac{\partial f}{\partial X_1} X_1 + \frac{\partial f}{\partial X_2} X_2. \tag{9.4}$$

Multiplying both sides of the above equation by product price yields:

$$PY = \text{MVP}_{X_1} X_1 + \text{MVP}_{X_2} X_2. \tag{9.5}$$

From (9.2) and (9.3) we learned profit maximization implies factors will be hired until their marginal value product is equal to their price. The right-hand side of (9.5) will thus be total cost, which will just equal total revenue. Paying each factor what it contributes will exhaust the value of output with no residual.

Market Imperfections

In this section we consider the effects on factor returns of imperfections in either the product or factor markets. We will first look at the product market, then the factor market, and finally a combination of both.

Monopoly in the Product Market

Impure competition in the product market implies that marginal revenue will not equal price, but rather:

$$\text{MR} = P(1 + 1/\eta), \tag{9.6}$$

where η is the elasticity of product demand.[4] Profit maximization now requires that the marginal revenue productivity (MR·MPP) denoted MRP_{X_i} of a factor be set equal to its price. In Figure 9.1*b*, given a

---

[4] Impure competition implies $\partial PY/\partial Y = P + Y(\partial P/\partial Y)$. Multiplying and dividing the right-hand term by P yields (9.6).

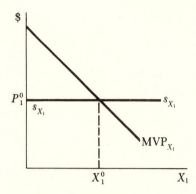

(*a*)   Pure Competition in Product and Factor Markets

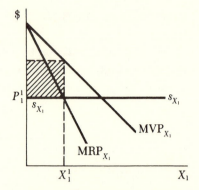

(*b*)   Impure Competition in Product Market, Pure Competition in Factor Market

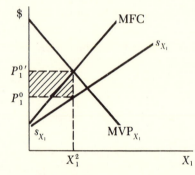

(*c*)   Pure Competition in Product Market, Impure Competition in Factor Market

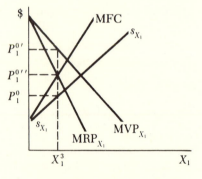

(*d*)   Impure Competition in Product and Factor Markets

Figure 9.1   Factor Market Conditions for a Firm. (*a*) Pure Competition in Product and Factor Markets; (*b*) Impure Competition in Product Market, Pure Competition in Factor Market; (*c*) Pure Competition in Product Market, Impure Competition in Factor Market; (*d*) Impure Competition in Product and Factor Markets.

supply schedule s_{X_1}, the profit-maximizing employment level will be X_1^1, less than with pure competition. At X_1^1 the MVP_{X_1} exceeds the price of X_1. If MVP_{X_1} is interpreted as society's valuation of the input's contribution, the factor receives a return less than its contribution to society. The return is, however, equal to the factor's contribution to the firm (MRP_{X_1}).

Monopsony in the Factor Market

Impure competition (monopsony) in the factor market implies a divergence between factor price and marginal factor cost. Given a total cost of X_1, P_1X_1, the marginal factor cost (MFC) will be:

$$\frac{\partial P_1 X_1}{\partial X_1} = P_1 + X_1 \frac{\partial P_1}{\partial X_1}. \tag{9.7}$$

Multiplying and dividing the right-hand term by P_1 yields:

$$\text{MFC} = P_1(1 + 1/e_1), \tag{9.8}$$

where e_1 is the elasticity of supply for X_1.

Monopsony exists when employers are able to discriminate in the factor market on the basis of wages or employment. Assuming the supply schedule is positively sloped ($\partial P_1/\partial X_1 > 0$), marginal factor cost (MFC) will exceed factor price or average cost as depicted in Figure 9.1c. Assuming pure competition in the product market, profit maximization implies equality of MVP and MFC, resulting in a level of employment of X_1^2. The return to the factor P_1^0 is determined by the supply schedule s_{X_1}. In this case the return is less than the factor's contribution (MVP_{X_1}).

"Exploitation"

The term "exploitation" has been frequently used and abused in economic writings. In this section we summarize three different meanings of the term. The implication of all three is that the factor receives less than it *should* or *ought* to get. In each case a different reference point for the wage is defined.

Marx

In Marx (1967) exploitation occurs when labor is paid a return less than the net value of its average product. Since the marginal productivity theory implies a real rate of return equal to one's marginal product, and, since the average product is declining in the area of rational operation for the firm, the marginal product will be less than the average product. According to Marx then "exploitation" is intrinsic to the competitive market system.[5]

Pigou

Consistent with his theory of externalities, Pigou (1932) sees "exploitation" as existing when factors are paid a return less than their marginal value product (MVP). One may interpret the latter as the societal valuation of the factor's contribution. It will exceed the firms valuation (MRP_{X_1}) when impure competition exists in the product market. Such a divergence does not necessarily imply, however, above-normal profits, and payments in excess of marginal revenue products are inconsistent with profit maximization.

In the Pigouian analysis, "exploitation" arises whenever the marginal social product of a factor exceeds its marginal private product. Using price as a measure of social value and marginal revenue as a measure of private value, impure competition in the product market implies "exploitation." Obviously, it can also occur given pure competition, since whenever positive externalities exist, a factor will be paid less than its value to society. In this case, and in the Marxian analysis, the firm is the exploiter. In the case of negative externalities, the factor is paid by the firm more than its contribution to society, and the factor is the "exploiter." The area of exploitation is shaded in Figure 9.1b.

E. H. Chamberlin

The analysis of "exploitation" with the broadest spectrum of acceptance owes its development to E. H. Chamberlin (1946), particularly in the later editions of the *Theory of Monopolistic Competition*. "Exploitation" is due to monopsony in the factor market. Assuming pure competition in the product market and profit maximization, firms will hire factors to the point where MVP equals the MFC, resulting in a level of employment of X_1^2 in Figure 9.1c. The return to the factor P_1^0 will be less than its contribution to the firm $P_1^{0'}$ (determined by the MVP schedule). Since the factor is paid less than it contributes to the firm,

---

[5] The following example will clarify the Marxian analysis. Assume a production function, with labor (X_1) the only variable input, and X_2 fixed at X_2^0. Pure competition exists in the product market. Production will take place in stage II, where the average product and marginal products of X_1 are declining, implying the marginal product schedule lies below the average product. Paying a factor a real return equal to its marginal product implies a return less than its average product.

the difference is available to the employer, who becomes the "exploiter." The shaded area in 9.1c is often referred to as the "bargaining area." The trade union movement in the United States is depicted as a struggle to win this area over to labor. Its division between labor and management is determined by the relative strength of the two parties.

Monopsony increases as the elasticity of substitution for the factor decreases. The latter may occur because of impediments to mobility or imperfect information among other reasons. Professional athletes with limited alternative careers and Mexican "braceros" are two very diverse examples of monopsonistic factor markets.

Figure 9.1d combines both the product and factor market. Its analysis will be left as an exercise. In our earlier discussions we concentrated on the allocational distortions due to market imperfections; now our concern is with the effects on factor returns. In assessing any market situation, both the allocation and distribution aspects must be studied.

Supply of Factors

Although each firm in a competitive market may perceive the supply of factors to be infinity elastic at the market price, factors are clearly not limitless in supply in the aggregate, and the services a particular factor can render are quite finite. We will restrict our discussion to the factor labor and ask what determines the volume of labor services, measured by hours worked, provided by an individual. Although there are some more novel approaches, our discussion will be along traditional neoclassical lines.

In the simplest case, we assume individuals maximize utility (U), which is determined by leisure time (L) and income (Y). The latter consists of wages at a constant rate (w) per hour and a return (r) on financial assets (A). Leisure time is the difference between total time (T) and time spent working. The problem may be formulated as the Lagrangian:

$$\max Z = U(L,Y) + \lambda[w(T - L) - rA - Y]. \qquad (9.9)$$

The first-order utility-maximizing conditions are then:

$$\frac{\partial U}{\partial L} - \lambda w = 0, \qquad (9.10)$$

$$\frac{\partial U}{\partial Y} - \lambda = 0, \tag{9.11}$$

$$w(T - L) - rA - Y = 0. \tag{9.12}$$

Assuming the second-order conditions are fulfilled, utility maximization implies the marginal rate of substitution between income and leisure equals the wage rate. From the above one can trace out the locus of utility-maximizing work times at various wages. As wages increase, leisure becomes relatively more costly so that work effort will rise (substitution effect). Since higher wages imply more income, (assuming leisure is not an inferior good), leisure time will also expand (income effect). As long as the substitution effect dominates, the individual's supply schedule will be positively sloped. The income effect is particularly important in the discussion of various welfare programs. Since such programs raise income, they provide a work disincentive. A great deal more will be said about this in the next chapter.

Our analysis could easily be extended to make the family the relevant decision-making unit. Particularly in the case of women, a distinction could be made between work in the home and that outside the home. As Becker (1965) points out, an alternative formulation of the utility function may be preferred in which utility is assumed a function of certain activities, each of which is in turn determined by market goods and time. Aggregation problems arise in deriving the market supply schedule in much the same way as in the case of demand. An hour's work effort is not homogeneous but very much a function of particular characteristics of an individual. The effect of these individual characteristics on the distribution of income is discussed in the next chapter.

Summary

At least in a competitive factor market, the return to the factor should reflect the marginal productivity. Many conditions can arise to alter the precision of this relation, but most economists would agree that earnings do measure, in some way, productive contribution. It would be difficult to elucidate all the possible distortions, but the following are among the more important. Discrimination against minorities (blacks, women, etc.) may imply wages less than productivity.[6] We have assumed labor is a variable input, and the employer will adjust the quantity to satisfy the profit-maximizing conditions. Certain kinds of workers may be more in the nature of fixed rather than variable inputs. Firms may make large investments in education and training. When production declines, workers may be kept on because the employer feels layoff would mean the permanent loss of his investment.[7] Labor unions are often assumed to be able to extract wages in excess of productivity from employers.[8] Empirically, it is very difficult to measure labor's marginal product since it involves all the problems associated with estimating a production function.[9] In the next chapter we will examine the distribution of income and the resultant inequalities.

References

Becker, G. S. 1965. "A Theory of the Allocation of Time," *Economic Journal* 75:493–527.

Bronfenbrenner, M. 1971. *Income Distribution Theory*. Chicago: Aldine.

Chamberlin, E. H. 1946. *The Theory of Monopolistic Competition*, 5th ed. Cambridge: Harvard University Press.

Ferguson, C. E. 1969. *The Neoclassical Theory of Production and Distribution*. New York: Cambridge University Press.

Hicks, J. R. 1963. The Theory of Wages, 2nd ed. London: Macmillan.

Layard, P. R. G., and A. A. Walters. 1978. *Micro-Economic Theory*. New York: McGraw-Hill.

Marshall, A. 1920. *Principles of Economics*, 8th ed. London: Macmillan.

Marx, K. 1967. *Capital*, 3 vols. ed. F. Engels, trans. S. Moore and E. Aveling, English ed. New York: International.

Pigou, A. C. 1932. *Economics of Welfare*, 4th ed. London: Macmillan.

Ricardo, D. 1951. *Principles of Political Economy*. In Piero Sraffa, ed., *Works and Correspondence of Daniel Ricardo*. Cambridge: Cambridge University Press.

---

[6] See: G. G. Cain, "The Challenge of Segmented Labor Market Theories to Orthodox Theory: A Survey," *Journal of Economic Literature* 14 (December 1976):1215–57.

[7] See: W. Oi, "Labor as a Quasi-Fixed Factor," *Journal of Political Economy* 70 (1962):538–55.

[8] See: J. F. O'Connell, "The Union Wage Effect: Differential Determinants and Differential Returns," *The Quarterly Review of Economics and Business* 20 (1980):107–17.

[9] Probably the most successful attempt in this direction is that by Thurow. See L. C. Thurow, "Disequilibrium and the Marginal Productivities of Capital and Labor," *The Review of Economics and Statistics* 45 (February 1968):23–31.

Chapter 10

PERSONAL DISTRIBUTION OF INCOME AND INCOME INEQUALITY

In the last chapter we derived earnings as a return to a factor of production, which arose because of the contribution the factor made in the productive process. An alternative approach is to attempt to explain wages by the characteristics of the recipients—in other words, to concentrate on the supply rather than the demand side. Two consequences follow from this approach: (1) the wage is viewed as a return to certain innate and acquired characteristics of individuals; (2) concern is now with wage or earning differences among individuals rather than between labor and other factors of production.

A Summary of the Distribution of Income

Many empirical studies have been done on the distribution of income in the United States and other countries. Despite numerous measurement and statistical problems, all agree that significant income inequality exists and persists.[1] Although our discussion will concentrate on income, it is also clear that the distribution of the stock of wealth in society is even more concentrated.[2] The extent of inequality can be

---

[1] The interested reader is referred to A. B. Atkinson (1975), Chiswick (1974), and Thurow (1975), among others.
[2] See for example, D. S. Proctor, "Survey of Financial Characteristics of Consumers," *Federal Reserve Bulletin* 50 (March 1967):285.

Table 10.1 Percentage Distribution of Income by Families

Year	Total families (1,000)	Under 2,500	2,500– 4,999	5,000– 7,499	7,500– 9,999	10,000– 12,499	12,500– 14,999	15,000– 19,999	20,000– 24,999	25,000– 34,999	35,000– 49,999	50,000 and over	Median Income
Current Dollars													
1950	39,929	33.7	43.1	15.8	4.2				3.2				3,319
1955	42,889	23.1	35.6	25.9	9.2	3.5	1.3	.6	.3		.5		4,418
1960[1]	45,539	17.5	24.5	28.4	15.2	7.5	3.1	2.1	.8		.9		5,620
1965[1]	48,509	12.4	19.2	24.1	19.0	11.9	5.8	4.6	1.5		1.4		6,957
1970[1]	52,227	6.6	12.5	15.2	16.6	15.8	11.0	13.1	4.6	3.0	1.1	.5	9,867
1975	56,245	3.5	8.5	10.6	10.6	11.4	10.9	18.8	11.6	9.5	3.2	1.4	13,719
1977	57,215	2.9	6.5	9.2	9.0	9.3	9.2	17.8	13.9	14.5	5.3	2.6	16,009
1978	57,804	2.6	5.6	7.8	8.1	8.5	8.2	16.9	14.5	17.6	6.7	3.6	17,640
1979[2]	58,385	2.2	4.7	6.4	7.1	8.3	7.3	15.0	14.4	19.2	10.3	5.2	19,684
Constant (1978) Dollars													
1950	39,929	10.0	10.2	14.9	15.3				49.6				10,008
1955	42,889	7.2	9.0	11.0	11.7	17.1	10.3	18.7	7.0	8.0			11,976
1960[1]	45,539	5.2	8.2	9.2	9.8	14.5	9.5	21.1	9.0	13.4			13,774
1965[1]	48,509	3.5	6.7	8.0	8.6	9.6	9.9	22.9	10.8	20.1			16,005
1970[1]	52,227	2.4	5.0	6.7	7.2	8.2	7.9	22.2	11.6	18.1	6.9	3.7	18,444
1975	56,245	2.5	4.6	7.4	7.8	8.1	8.1	16.5	14.7	19.3	7.3	3.8	18,502
1977	57,215	2.5	4.4	7.1	7.6	7.6	7.7	15.7	14.4	20.5	8.1	4.5	19,176
1978	57,804	2.4	4.6	6.6	7.2	7.6	7.5	15.3	14.8	20.7	8.4	4.9	19,626
1979[2]	58,385	2.2	4.7	6.4	7.1	8.3	7.3	15.0	14.4	19.2	10.3	5.2	19,684

Source: U.S. Bureau of the Census, *Current Population Reports*, Series P-60, No. 125.

[1] Data for "all families" revised using population controls based on the 1970 Census of Population.

[2] Based on householder concept. Restricted to primary families; see source.

observed from inspection of Tables 10.1 and 10.2. In the former, the distribution of family income since 1950 is presented. Although median family income has clearly increased in both current and constant terms, and the proportion of families in the lower end of the distribution has declined, income inequality is still significant. Table 10.2 reports individuals with incomes less than that required for a minimum standard of living. Although there has been a 43 percent reduction for whites in the incidence of poverty, the decline for blacks has been less dramatic (34 percent). Despite these reductions, the number of individuals who remain in povery is still unacceptably large.

Theory of Human Capital

In the last chapter we stressed the importance of an individual's contribution to production in determining income, but this explanation is by no means the only one for the distribution of income in society. Sahota (1978) provides an excellent summary of alternative theories and the controversies surrounding them. If an individual is paid an amount related to his or her productivity, we must now ask what personal characteristics render an individual productive. We will use the framework generally associated with human capital theory, which was originated by T. W. Schultz (1960, 1971) and Jacob Mincer (1958, 1974).

Although traditional neoclassical production theory assumes a short-run time frame, the view that labor is a form of capital implies the long run. The wage is a return to human capital accumulation attained through education, training, occupational choice, geographic location, health, and so forth. The fundamentals of the human capital approach can be seen with the help of the following simple example. Denote earnings in time t by w_t and assume our investment of C dollars is made in time $t - 1$. The rate of return is assumed a constant r. The earnings function can then be expressed as:

$$w_t = w_{t-1} e^{rC_{t-1}} + u_t, \qquad (10.1)$$

where u_t is a random error term accounting for unsystematic transitory changes in earnings. Rewriting the above in logs yields:

$$\ln w_t = \ln w_0 + r \sum_{j=1}^{t-1} C_{t-j} + u_t', \qquad (10.2)$$

Table 10.2   Persons Below the Poverty Level by Race 1960–1978

Year	Total		White		Black	
	Number (in thousands)	Percent	Number (in thousands)	Percent	Number (in thousands)	Percent
1960	39,851	22.2	28,309	17.8	11,542	55.9
1961	39,628	21.9	27,890	17.4	11,738	56.1
1962	38,625	21.0	26,672	16.4	11,953	55.8
1963	36,436	19.5	25,238	15.3	11,198	51.0
1964	36,055	19.0	24,957	14.9	11,098	49.6
1965[4]	33,185	17.3	22,496	13.3	10,689	47.1
1966[1]	28,510	14.7	19,290	11.3	8,867	41.8
1967	27,769	14.2	18,983	11.0	8,486	39.3
1968	25,389	12.8	17,395	10.0	7,616	34.7
1969	24,289	12.2	16,671	9.5	7,215	32.3
1969[2]	24,147	12.1	16,659	9.5	7,095	32.2
1970	25,420	12.6	17,484	9.9	7,548	33.5
1971	25,559	12.5	17,780	9.9	7,396	32.5
1972	24,460	11.9	16,203	9.0	7,710	33.3
1973	22,973	11.1	15,142	8.4	7,388	31.4
1974	24,260	11.6	16,290	8.9	7,467	31.4
1974[3]	23,370	11.2	15,736	8.6	7,182	30.3
1975	25,877	12.3	17,770	9.7	7,545	31.3
1976	24,975	11.8	16,713	9.1	7,595	31.1
1977	24,720	11.6	16,416	8.9	7,726	31.3
1978	24,497	11.4	16,259	8.7	7,625	30.6

Source: Department of Commerce, Bureau of the Census, *Current Population Reports,* Series P-60, Nos. 115 and 116. (Persons were classified as poor or nonpoor by using income thresholds adopted by a federal interagency committee in 1969. These thresholds vary by family size, composition, and residence—farm or nonfarm.)

[1] Beginning in 1966, data are based on revised methodology for processing income data.
[2] Beginning in 1969, data are based on 1970 census population controls and therefore are not strictly comparable with data for earlier years.
[3] Beginning in 1974, data are based on revised methodology for processing income data. See *Current Population Reports,* Series P-60, No. 103.
[4] Data for 1960–1965 are for black and other races. Blacks represent approximately 90 percent of the black and other category for these years.

where w_0 is the wage in the absence of any investment and

$$\sum_{j=1}^{t-1} c_{t-j}$$

is the cumulative investment. From (10.2) one can roughly group the determinants of earnings into three categories: (1) innate factors such as intelligence, manual dexterity, etc. affecting w_0; (2) acquired abilities through investments in education, experience, on the job training, etc.; (3) a random component due to transitory, stochastic factors.

Some would argue that a person's well-being is determined by fate, that luck or chance determines one's lot. Such an approach stresses the random component of earnings and is generally formulated in terms of a first-order Markov process of the form:

$$w_t = w_{t-1} + u_t = w_0 + \sum_{j=1}^{t} u_{t-j}. \tag{10.3}$$

One of the implications of a Markov process is that over time the distribution of earnings would approach a long-run equilibrium or steady state, which could be derived from information on the current income distribution and that in the immediately preceding period. Although the simplicity of this approach is at first glance appealing, it provides little insight into policies appropriate for altering earnings patterns.

The human capital theory assumes individuals have control over their earnings and act in a way to maximize their return. This implies policies can be introduced to alter investment and thereby earnings. Mincer (1974) concludes that half of the inequality in earnings is attributable to investment in schooling and subsequent training. Sahota (1978), among others, points out, however, that this might be an upwardly biased estimate since human capital theorists have failed to consider the effects of "preschool" and individual rather than "formal" kinds of investment. Although most economists would agree that education can affect earnings, there is some dispute over whether it does so by directly influencing productivity or whether it simply provides the credentials for entry into a higher-earnings bracket.

Thurow (1975) hypothesizes that productivity derives not from individual characteristics but from job characteristics. An individual is not productive in the abstract—only with reference to a particular job. In such a context, education and similar human capital attributes may serve as "signals" or "screening" devices to potential employers. As Spence (1973) and Stiglitz (1975) point out, employers have little knowledge of prospective employees' abilities prior to hiring. By using information on education, training, and similar characteristics, employers are able to filter out applicants until the ones with the greatest likelihood of being able to perform a particular job are hired.

Implications for Income Distribution

Human capital theory provides an explanation of individual earnings at a point in time. By making inferences about the future, the methodology of control theory, used earlier in the context of dynamic optimization, allows us to examine earnings distributions over time. The argument developed below draws heavily on that of Blinder (1974).

Letting the family be the decision-making unit, consider a utility function additively separable in consumption (C) and leisure (L). The marginal utility of both functions denoted $U(\cdot)$ and $V(\cdot)$, respectively, is positive but diminishing. The family also desires to leave an inheritance for future generations equal to $(1 - \tau)K_T$, where K_T is the terminal value of accumulated nonhuman capital, and τ the rate of inheritance taxation. The utility of the bequest will be denoted $B(\cdot)$. Beginning at t_0, and assuming a lifetime of T years, the utility function can be represented as:

$$\int_{t_0}^{T} e^{-pt} [U(C) + V(L)]dt + B[(1 - \tau)K], \tag{10.4}$$

where p is the time rate of discount.

Constraints on consumption take two forms. Consumption (C) plus savings (S) in any time period must equal the wage after tax (w) times hours worked (H) plus the after-tax rate of return (r) on capital:

$$C(t) + s(t) = w(t)H(t) + rK(t). \tag{10.5}$$

In this simplest of cases, wages are assumed given rather than endogenously determined.

The second constraint requires that the rate of capital accumulation $[\overset{o}{K}(t)]$ equal savings:

$$\overset{\circ}{K}(t) = s(t). \tag{10.6}$$

Equation (10.5) can be solved for $C(t)$ and substituted into (10.4) having the single constraint (10.6). The two control variables will be s and H, and the Hamiltonian can be expressed as:

$$Z(K,s,H) = e^{-pt} U(rK + wH - s) + e^{-pt} V(T - H) + \lambda(t)s; \tag{10.7}$$

where λ is the "shadow price" or marginal value of savings. Given strict concavity of $V(\cdot)$, and $B(\cdot)$, the first-order conditions for a maximum are:

$$\frac{\partial Z}{\partial K} = -\overset{\circ}{\lambda}(t) = rU'(C) e^{-pt}, \tag{10.8}$$

$$\frac{\partial Z}{\partial s} = -U'(C)e^{-pt} + \lambda(t) = 0, \tag{10.9}$$

$$\frac{\partial Z}{\partial H} = -e^{-pt} V'(L) + e^{-pt}U'(C)w \leq 0, \tag{10.10}$$

with $<$ implying $H = 0$.

The transversality condition is:

$$\lambda(t) = \frac{dB[(1 - \tau)K_T]}{dK_T}. \tag{10.11}$$

From (10.10) with H positive, maximization requires:

$$\frac{V'(L)}{U'(C)} = w(t), \tag{10.12}$$

the marginal rate of substitution between leisure and consumption should equal the wage rate. This is similar to the comparative static conclusion, though now the variables are functions of time. Differentiating (10.12) logarithmically with respect to time for positive H yields:

$$\frac{LV''(L)}{V'(L)} \cdot \frac{\overset{\circ}{L}}{L} - \frac{CU''(C)}{U'(C)} \cdot \frac{\overset{\circ}{C}}{C} = \frac{\overset{\circ}{w}}{w}. \tag{10.13}$$

In our earlier discussion of optimal control, it was shown that:

$$\frac{CU''(C)}{U'(C)} \cdot \frac{\overset{o}{C}}{C} = r - p,^3$$

and denoting $LV''(L)/V'(L)$ as ξ, (10.13) can be rewritten as:

$$\frac{\overset{o}{L}}{L} = \frac{r - p - m(t)}{\xi}, \tag{10.14}$$

where $m(t)$ is the rate of growth of wages at time t.

From (10.13) one can infer the behavior of earnings over time. It will depend on work time (leisure time), which will vary with the net return on capital (r), the time rate of discount (p), the rate of change in wage (m), and the rate of change in the marginal utility of leisure (ξ). Other things equal, a low time preference implies concentration of work in the early stages of life and just the opposite for a high time preference.

From (10.10) H will be zero ("retirement") when:

$$w(t)U'(C) < V'(L). \tag{10.15}$$

The term on the left can be thought of as the marginal utility of the wage. If it declines over time, retirement will occur at the end of one's life; if it increases, the opposite happens. By postulating certain initial conditions and assumptions, we can trace out the income distribution over a person's (or family's) life, and also distributions among individuals.

In the next chapter we will consider policies to alter the personal distribution of income to achieve greater social welfare.

References

Atkinson, A. B. 1975. *The Economics of Inequality*. London: Oxford University Press.
Blinder, A. S. 1974. *Toward an Economic Theory of Income Distribution*. Cambridge, Mass.: M.I.T. Press.
Champernowne, D. G. 1973. *The Distribution of Income Between Persons*. New York: Cambridge University Press.
Chiswick, B. R. 1974. *Income Inequality*. New York: National Bureau of Economic Research.

---

[3] See Chapter 8 for a review of the conditions required for dynamic optimization.

Mincer, J. 1958. "Investment in Human Capital and Personal Income Distribution." *Journal of Political Economy* 66(4):281–302.

———. 1974. *Schooling, Experience and Earnings*. New York: National Bureau of Economic Research.

Sahota, G. S. 1978. "Theories of Personal Income Distribution: A Survey." *Journal of Economic Literature* 16:1–55.

Schultz, T. W. 1960. "Capital Formulation by Education." *Journal of Political Economy* 68(6):571–83.

———. 1971. *Investment in Human Capital*. New York: Free Press.

Spence, A. M. 1973. "Job Market Signaling." *Quarterly Journal of Economics* 87(3):355–74.

———. 1974. *Market Signaling*. Cambridge, Mass.: Harvard University Press.

Stiglitz, J. E. 1975. "The Theory of 'Screening' Education and the Distribution of Income." *American Economic Review* 65:283–300.

Thurow, L. C. 1975. *Generating Inequality*. New York: Basic Books.

Supplementary Readings

Becker, G. S. 1967. *Human Capital*. New York: National Bureau of Economic Research.

Chiswick, B. R., and J. A. O'Neill. 1977. *Human Resources and Income Distribution*. New York: Norton and Co.

Chapter 11

EQUITY IN THE DISTRIBUTION OF INCOME

From the previous chapter, it should be clear that the ultimate distribution of income is affected by many factors: tastes and preferences, initial endowments of human and nonhuman capital, the rate of interest, the time rate of discount, and the growth rate of earnings. The myriad of government programs that influence, directly or indirectly, incomes gives clear indication that society perceives income distribution as affecting social welfare. The specific rationale or objective underlying particular policies is more difficult to derive, but more will be said about this later.

Kinds of Redistribution Policies

There appear to be two general approaches to the realization of greater equality in income distribution. At one extreme are policies directed at *specific* segments of the population. Examples are subsidized housing for the elderly, aid to families with dependent children (AFDC), food stamps, and many manpower retraining programs. At the other extreme are more *general* programs in which income or wage levels are the exclusive determinant for eligibility. Newer proposals such as the Negative Income Tax (NIT) and the Negative Wage Tax (NWT) can be cited as examples.

Current System

Table 11.1 summarizes the major federal income maintenance programs. Musgrave and Musgrave (1973) estimate that in 1970 approximately one-half of the needy people received some form of support. Those not covered consisted primarily of non-aged individuals and couples, particularly in the latter case those without children, and persons in families headed by a full-time worker. The programs listed in Table 11.1 necessitate the identification of particular groups in society, and in part because of this labeling requirement, implementation

Table 11.1   Income Security (In millions of dollars)

Program	Outlays Under Existing Laws		
	1980 actual	1981 estimate	1982 estimate
General retirement and disability insurance			
Old-age, survivors and disability insurance	115,997	131,048	150,145
Railroad Retirement	4,400	4,848	5,384
Other	1,865	1,916	1,895
Subtotal	122,262	137,812	157,424
Federal employee and retirement, disability and workers compensation	24,732	28,263	31,007
Unemployment insurance	17,703	22,575	25,988
Public assistance and other supplements			
Supplemental security income	6,468	7,278	7,983
AFDC and related assistance	7,709	7,728	6,263
Housing assistance	27,813	30,870	31,386
Food stamps	9,182	11,084	12,882
School lunch and other nutrition programs	4,592	4,999	6,094
Earned income credit payments	1,275	1,203	1,115
Other	2,462	3,341	1,365
Subtotal, public assistance and other income supplements	59,501	66,503	67,088
Total	224,198	255,153	281,507

Source: U.S. Office of Management and Budget, *Budget of the United States Government Fiscal Year 1982* (Washington: U.S. Government Printing Office, 1981), p. 251.

and administrative costs tend to be high.[1] Another criticism frequently directed at redistribution programs is that they lessen the incentive to work on the part of societal members.[2] With the help of Figure 11.1 we will discuss a number of income redistribution plans and their effects on work incentives. Income net of taxes and transfers is measured vertically and earnings, horizontally. In the absence of any tax or transfer program, earnings and income would be identical, as measured by the 45° line *OD*.

Lump-Sum Transfers

Consider the simplest program in which anyone whose earnings are below some minimum acceptable living standard (*OS'* in Figure 11.1) is given a lump-sum transfer equal to *OS*. Total income received will follow a path *SABD*. Earnings up to *OS'* are not taxed, while the next

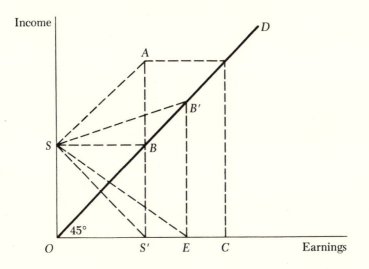

Figure 11.1   Income Supplements

---

[1] A program like AFDC requires the husband not be living with the family. Such a provision is difficult to police and fosters the disruption of many family units.
[2] Though we will concentrate on the disincentive effect on recipients, the higher tax payments required to finance such programs may also lessen the work incentive of other members of society. See, for example, J. F. O'Connell, "Multiple Job Holding and Marginal Tax Rates," *National Tax Journal* 32 (Match 1979):73–76.

dollar is taxed an amount equal to *OS*. Earnings must increase to *OC* without the transfer before the individual is as well off as at *S'*.

100 Percent Marginal Tax Rates

One might view as more equitable a scheme that provides transfers equal to the difference between the minimum standard (*OS*) and one's earnings. In this case, the subsidy would follow the path *SS'*, while income would increase along *SBD*. Over the interval *OS'*, a dollar in subsidy is lost for each dollar earned, thus imposing a 100 percent marginal tax rate.

Negative Income Tax (NIT)

Both the above schemes provide strong disincentives to work. In the first case, there is a disincentive to have earnings in excess of *OS'*, and in the second, for earnings less than *OS'*. Under the NIT, all families would be assured an income *OS*. Income would then expand given earnings along a ray such as *SB'D*. As earnings increase, the subsidy would decline but less than dollar for dollar as indicated by *SE*. Earnings over the interval *OE* would be taxed at a high (sometimes assumed 50 percent) but considerably less than a 100 percent rate. If the tax rate were 50 percent, *OE* would be twice *OS'*. Since the NIT applies to all individuals, and since even those with earnings in excess of *OS* are subsidized, its cost will tend to be higher than with a 100 percent marginal rate. The NIT does reduce disincentives, but Blinder (1974), using simulations, shows that for a number of fiscally feasible schemes, the NIT will have relatively little effect on the distribution of income.

Disincentive Effects

Figure 11.2 illustrates the effects of the above programs on work effort. Utility is assumed a function of income and leisure, with the former measured vertically and the latter horizontally (total available time is denoted *T*). In the absence of any tax or revenue program, the wage will equal the negative of the slope of line *AT*, and utility maximization will occur at *B* with L^0 hours of leisure and $T - L^0$ hours of work. Assume Y^0 is considered by society to be unacceptably low, and a transfer

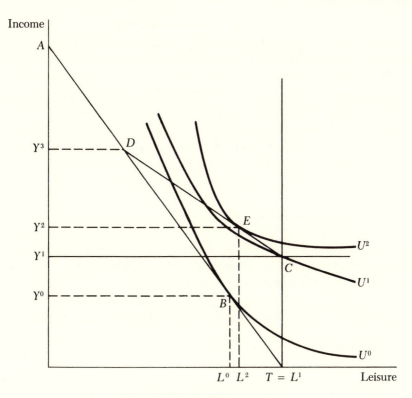

Figure 11.2   Work Disincentives

is given that increases income to Y^1. The new utility-maximizing position will occur at C, with a resultant decrease in work effort $(T - L^1)$. In this case the effects on work effort are similar whether the transfer be of the lump-sum variety or the 100 percent marginal tax rate variety.

A negative income tax will change the slope of the price line. Now between incomes Y^1 and Y^3 the individual can maintain some of his or her earnings in addition to receiving the transfer. The negative of the slope of CD represents the after-tax wage, $(1 - t)w$, where the tax rate (t) is assumed to be 50 percent. The new utility-maximizing position will be at E, with both income (Y^2) and work effort $(T - L^2)$ increased. Figure 11.2 clearly shows that with the NIT all individuals with incomes less than Y^3 will be subsidized—many more than in a simple transfer scheme. This additional cost will at least in part be offset by the resultant increase in employment and output. Also, as the marginal tax rate is reduced to stimulate work effort, the income levels subsidized increase.

If utility functions are well behaved, it can be argued that relative to a simple transfer, the NIT will increase work effort. What is not clear, however, is whether work effort will be greater or less than it would be in the absence of any program.

A number of experiments have been performed with various income maintenance schemes. The results of their implementation in rural areas of North Carolina and Iowa are summarized by Palmer and Pechman (1978), and Pechman and Timpane (1975) examine the results of a study of urban workers in New Jersey.

Negative Wage Tax (NWT)

Relative to programs imposing marginal tax rates of 100 percent, or simple transfers, the NIT provides a greater work incentive. However, given the tax rates required to finance the NIT, the after-tax wage is still considerably less than it would be in the absence of any program. Figure 11.3 depicts the labor market for low-income earners. The

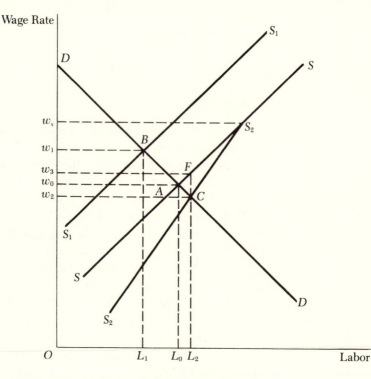

Figure 11.3   Negative Wage Tax

competitive wage is w_0, with an employment level L_0. Earned income will be Ow_0AL_0, and assuming a single-variable production function, national income will be $ODAL_0$.

The NIT will shift the supply toward the origin denoted by S_1S_1. At the new equilibrium, national income is $ODBL_1$, and earned income Ow_1BL_1. The elasticity of demand will determine the effect of the plan on earned income. Its cost includes not only the actual transfers but also the loss in national income due to reduced employment relative to no plan. In cases where complementary and substitutability of factors are allowed, the lost employment to the former and the gain to the latter would also have to be considered.

Wage subsidy programs (NWT) such as those proposed by J. Kesselman (1971), E. Browning (1973), and Blinder (1974) have two advantages. First, they reduce even more than the NIT the disincentive effects associated with high marginal tax rates. Second, Blinder shows that such proposals provide much greater potential for income redistribution. Under NWT proposals, the subsidy would vary inversely with the wage rate. Everyone with a wage (w) less than some specified value (w_s) would be subsidized at a rate (s). The total subsidy to any individual (S) would be

$$S = s(w_s - w) \qquad \text{for } w < w_s, \qquad (11.1)$$
$$= \quad\ 0 \qquad \text{for } w \geq w_s.$$

In Figure 11.3, a NWT will shift the supply schedule to S_2S_2S with the following consequences. Individuals will work more at a given wage than previously because their net wage will be higher. The subsidy per labor unit will equal the difference between SS and S_2S_2. Because of the increase in employment, national income expands, which makes the burden of the program less than the transfer cost. The new equilibrium will be at C, with a market wage w_2 and subsidized wage w_3. The transfer cost will be w_2w_3FC, while national income increases by L_0ACL_2.

Obviously, the NWT assists only the working poor and would have to be supplemented with other programs. Second, the connection between wage and living standards may not be as clear as that between the latter and income. For example, it may be the case that the wages of many teenagers are low, justifying subsidization, while their family income exceeds the determined minimum. NIT and NWT programs were originally thought desirable because of the problems associated with identifying those eligible for many current benefits. G. Akerloff

(1978) has recently argued that optimality may require a combination of programs, some with general application and others requiring more precise identification or "tagging." Obviously, if among those with incomes or wages less than the stated minimum only a fraction are in need, assisting only those will reduce cost, provided identification costs are low.

The willingness of the wealthy to provide income supplements to the poor implies some degree of redistribution that has advantages for both those who contribute (the rich) and the recipients (the poor). Following an argument developed by Zeckhauser (1971), the improvement of the poor can be thought of as an externality entering the utility function of the rich. Obviously, the rich would prefer low-cost programs that provide the poor with work incentives. The utility function of the rich (U_r) will be determined by the income of the poor (Y), their hours worked (H), and the cost of the program per poor person (C).

$$U_r = U_r(Y,H,C), \qquad (11.2)$$

where

$$\frac{\partial U_r}{\partial Y} > 0, \ \frac{\partial U_r}{\partial H} > 0, \ \frac{\partial U_r}{\partial C} < 0.$$

The directions of the indicated effects are assumed to hold only within ranges. Some work requirements, such as forced child labor, may be odious to the rich. Similarly, very high incomes for the poor may threaten the position of the rich.

The utility of the poor (U_p) is assumed a function of their income (Y) and leisure (or its assumed opposite, work):

$$U_p = U_p(Y,H), \qquad (11.3)$$

where

$$\frac{\partial U_p}{\partial Y} > 0, \ \text{and} \ \frac{\partial U_p}{\partial H} < 0.$$

With no administrative costs, the cost per person of a redistribution program (C) will equal the income of the poor less hours worked at an assumed wage (w). Considering a very simple two-person economy, in which the rich and poor are weighted equally, the social welfare function may be formulated as:

$$W = U_r(Y,H,C) + U_p(Y,H) + \lambda[C - Y + wH]. \qquad (11.4)$$

The first-order maximizing conditions require that:

$$\frac{\partial U_r}{\partial Y} + \frac{\partial U_p}{\partial Y} - \lambda = 0, \qquad (11.5)$$

$$\frac{\partial U_r}{\partial H} + \frac{\partial U_p}{\partial H} + \lambda w = 0, \qquad (11.6)$$

$$\frac{\partial U_r}{\partial C} + \lambda = 0. \qquad (11.7)$$

From 11.5 it is obvious that the Lagrangian (λ) is the marginal social utility of income to the poor. From (11.7) it must equal the loss or cost of redistribution to the rich. From (11.6) the poor should work until the disutility of their working just equals the negative of the marginal utility of their working to the rich and the negative of the marginal social utility of the wage.

It is unlikely that free trade exists among the members of our fictitious society. As Zeckhauser points out, it is more reasonable to assume the redistribution program is established by the rich, and the poor respond not unlike a leader-follower arrangement. Figure 11.4 illustrates the nature of the problem; after-transfer income of the poor is measured vertically and hours worked by the poor, horizontally. The line *OD* measures income from earnings, its slope being the wage rate. First assume a minimum income *OS* is established, with a 100 percent marginal tax rate, so that income will follow *SBD*. Given an indifference map represented by U^0, U^1, U^2, utility maximization for the poor will occur at *S* where there is no work effort.

Consider now a negative income tax scheme depicted by *SB'D*. Utility maximization will now be at *C* with higher utility, income, and greater work effort. The cost per person of the plan will equal the vertical distance *CA*. The rich choose the minimum income level *S* and the marginal tax rate (determined by the slope of *SB'*). The poor respond by choosing *H* to maximize U_p. The income of the poor will be:

$$Y = S + w(1 - t)H, \qquad (11.8)$$

while the cost of the program is:

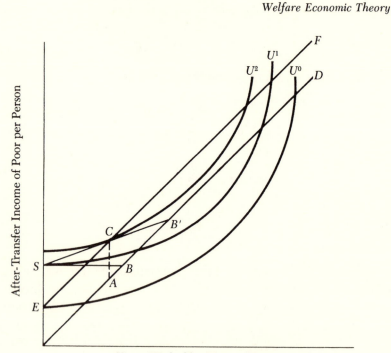

Figure 11.4   Costs and Benefits of Income Supplements

$$C = S - Hwt, \tag{11.9}$$

where H is the utility-maximizing response by the poor. The line EF
parallel to OD through C represents the locus of alternative plans
(value of S and t) having a cost CA. From all the alternatives, the rich
choose the utility maximizing one.

Some would argue that if indeed the rich benefit from the well-being
of the poor, redistribution would occur voluntarily without government
coercion. How much philanthropic giving would occur in the absence
of government programs is difficult to say, but such an approach poses
some serious problems. First, in the above formulation both the income of the poor and hours worked were arguments. One wonders
how in a voluntary system a work requirement could be imposed.
Second, it would be to the benefit of any rich person to have the others
but not himself give to the poor. A government program can lessen the
likelihood of this *free-rider* problem.

Summary

This concludes our discussion of income distribution. Although the concept of efficiency was quite straightforward, that of equity tends to be more value laden and subjective. In the same way that the conditions for efficiency followed from the objective function being maximized, so too policies for redistribution require the formulation of a preference order for society. In Chapter 3 we assumed the existence of a social welfare function, but we must now examine more closely the issues involved in arriving at social choices.

References

Akerloff, G. A. 1978. "The Economics of Tagging." *American Economic Review* 68(1):8–19.

Blinder, A. S. 1974. *Toward an Economic Theory of Income Distribution.* Cambridge, Mass.: MIT Press.

Browning, E. 1971. "Incentive and Disincentive Experimentation for Income Maintenance Policy Purposes: Note." *American Economic Review* 61:707–18.

———. 1973. "Alternative Programs for Income Redistribution: The NIT and the NWT." *American Economic Review* 63(1):38–49.

Kesselman, J. 1971. "Conditional Subsidies in Income Maintenance." *Western Economic Journal* 4:1–20.

Musgrave, R. A., and P. B. Musgrave. 1973. *Public Finance in Theory and Practice.* New York: McGraw-Hill.

Palmer, J. L., and J. A. Pechman, ed. 1978. *Welfare in Rural Areas: The North Carolina-Iowa Income Maintenance Experiment.* Washington: Brookings Institute.

Pechman, J. A., and P. M. Timpane, eds. 1975. *Work Incentives and Income Guarantees: The New Jersey Negative Income Tax Experiment:* Washington: Brookings Institute.

Zeckhauser, R. J. 1971. "Optimal Mechanism for Income Transfer," *American Economic Review* 61:324–34.

Chapter 12

SOCIAL CHOICE AND COLLECTIVE DECISION MAKING

Until now we have ignored the question of whether it is possible to represent accurately the collective preferences of the members of a social unit. In Chapter 3 we found that to choose among alternative Pareto efficient points some decision had to be made concerning the distribution of utility among society's members. The introduction of the social welfare function (SWF) allowed us to derive a unique optimizing solution, but at the cost of a great deal of controversy. Although literature on social choice has grown exponentially over the recent past, one of the first to address the existence and properties of social welfare functions was Kenneth Arrow in a work entitled *Social Choice and Individual Values* (1951). Since his treatment still serves as the focal point in the debate, our discussion will center around it.

Group Welfare

The transition from individual to collective welfare is by no means an easy or smooth one. Two factors are primarily responsible for the problems. First, utility in most economic discussions is assumed not measurable in a cardinal sense, so that one cannot precisely quantify individual satisfaction. Second, utility is not comparable between individuals, precluding interpersonal comparisons. The absence of cardinal measurability implies one is unable to affix a meaningful measure of how much one commodity bundle is preferred to another by an individual. Levels of utility cannot be measured on a ratio scale, and, since the utility one person derives from a commodity bundle cannot be compared with the utility of another person, one cannot add individual utilities and arrive at some measure of total collective satisfaction. This inability to compare utilities becomes an even more serious problem when we allow for the possibility of interactions among preference functions.

A former colleague of mine would suggest I conclude my discussion of social choice here. He would argue that the difficulties in formulating a collective preference function are such that the benefits derived from such intellectual endeavors are less than the costs. I might add that both costs and benefits are measured in expected value terms. Yet failure to address the problem renders it no less real, and as society becomes more and more interdependent, and as resources become more and more scarce, the need for some measure of the collective will or preference grows.

One might for a moment speculate about ways of solving the problem. One device is to assume a benevolent dictator, who paternalistically imposes his will on the community. Individual preferences are disregarded, and the collective preference becomes that of the dominant individual. An alternative might be to pursue those policies that improve the utility of at least one person without making anyone else worse off. This choice avoids the need for interpersonal utility comparisons but as such precludes consideration of policies in which some individuals gain and others lose. As discussed earlier this is known as the "Pareto criterion" and is implicit in a perfectly competitive economy in the long run.

Finally, one might devise a weighting scheme and a common *numeraire* or denominator of individual preferences that would permit additivity and comparability. In the market the system of prices and measures, such as national income or per capita income, are movements in this direction. Politically, in a democratic society, the voting mechanism performs an analogous function.

Properties of Social Orderings

More scientifically than the above, we could ask what properties a social welfare function should satisfy, and then whether it is possible to devise such a collective ordering. Arrow hypothesizes two axioms and five conditions to be met by such a social ordering. The axioms correspond to the combined properties of completeness and reflexity, which Arrow refers to as *connectedness*, and transitivity. Although we defined these terms earlier in the context of individual preferences, the interpretation is quite different now since we are concerned with ethical judgments of alternative social states. The following are the five conditions:

1. Given some admissible set of individual orderings of all alternatives, every logically possible set of individual orderings of a certain set of alternatives can be derived. An "admissible" set of individual orderings is one for which the social ordering defines a corresponding social relation. The domain of the welfare function includes all logically possible individual orderings (i.e., for every individual ordering we should be able to derive the corresponding social order). In his original formulation, Arrow assumed that there were at least three alternatives for which all possible individual orderings are admissible. For this reason the three alternatives are sometimes referred to as the "Free Triple." The condition was later extended notably by Blau (1957) to the "Free Orderings," implying all logically possible orderings are admissible. The importance of such an assumption is obvious. If all individuals have the same or very similar preferences, the problem of a collective preference ceases to exist since it will be the same as that of each individual. The social ordering should be universal in the sense of derivable from any logically possible set of individual orderings.

2. There is a nonnegative association between changes in individual and societal preferences. If an individual's position improves, that of society cannot worsen. Little more need be said about condition 2.

3. The third condition is referred to as the "independence of irrelevant alternatives." The choice made from a given environment or set of alternatives should depend only on the choices in that set. If one of the alternatives is eliminated it should not affect the ordering of those that remain.[1]

---

[1] An example from Arrow of a case where this condition is not fulfilled may be helpful. Assume there are three voters (1,2,3) and four candidates (W,X,Y,Z). Each voter ranks the candidates assuming weights equal to 4 for the first choice and 1 for the fourth. The orderings are as follows: X,Y,Z,W; X,Y,Z,W; Z,W,X,Y. Adding the weights between voters gives X 10, Z 8, Y 7, and W 5. Candidate Y withdraws from the race and voter 1 now assigns 3 to Z and 2 to W. The other voters adjust similarly. Now X and Z both have a value of 10, despite the fact that Y was considered inferior to X by all voters. Our preference function should avoid such ambiguities.

4. The social welfare function is not imposed. It is imposed when for some set of alternatives the social preference is set independently of the individual members of society. This would occur in cases where even though the members of society have the ordering *ARB*, society ranks *BRA*.

5. No one individual can alone determine the social ordering. Were such an individual to exist, he or she would be a dictator, and his or her absence is referred to by Arrow as the "condition of nondictatorship."

The distinction between conditions 4 and 5 may not appear obvious at first glance. The former prevents someone from outside imposing preferences on society. The latter prevents a single member of society from determining the social preference.

Arrow's Impossibility Theorem

In the general case of at least three alternatives, Arrow shows that every social welfare function satisfying conditions 2 and 3 and the two axioms must either be imposed or dictatorial (violate conditions 4 and 5). Conditions 2 and 3 suffice to exclude interpersonal utility comparisons either cardinally or ordinally. The only generally acceptable social ordering, excluding interpersonal comparisons, is thus either imposed or dictatorial.

Sketch of a Proof

The proof of Arrow's conclusions is based on the notion of a "decisive set." A set of voters is decisive in establishing a social preference of *A* over *B* if their ranking of *A* over *B* is sufficient to establish a social ranking of *A* over *B*, regardless of the preferences of other members of the set.

Let *V* be the smallest of all decisive sets of *S* for *A* over *B*. Divide *V* into V_1, a single individual, and V_2, consisting of all other members of *V*. V_3 represents all persons in *S* not in *V*. None of the sets is assumed empty. Suppose the following orderings exist for the three sets (where *P* refers to strict preference and *I* to indifference): V_1: *APBPC*; V_2: *CPAPB*; V_3: *BPCPA*. Since V_1 and V_2 prefer *A* to *B*, this is sufficient to establish the social ordering. V_2 has the ordering *CPB*, while V_1 and V_3

have *BPC*. If the social ordering is *CPB*, then V_2 is decisive. By assumption it is not decisive, therefore, either for society *BPC* or *BIC*. In either case axiom 2 (transitivity) requires *APC* (*APB*, *BPC*, then *APC*). Yet only V_1 prefers *A* to *C*, thus V_1 must be a dictator. This approach is used by Arrow to demonstrate the general impossibility of satisfying the two axioms and five conditions deemed desirable for the social ordering.[2]

Possible Compromises

Although it may not be possible to satisfy all the prerequisites set forth by Arrow, the need for a collective expression of preferences is sufficiently important to examine how close we can come, or what compromises must be made to arrive at a welfare function. First, welfare functions are not impossible if we allow for cardinality and interpersonal utility comparisons. Under such circumstances, we could simply add individual preferences to arrive at the aggregate or collective preference. What we would like, however, is to find the minimum compromise necessary to ensure a well-behaved social ordering. Since most such efforts involve the property of transitivity, we will concentrate our discussion on that subject.

Transitivity

A social relation *R* ("at least as preferred as") is transitive if for three alternatives *A*,*B*, and *C*, *ARB* and *BRC*, then *ARC*.[3] Although transitivity is a necessary prerequisite for individual rationality, Plott (1971) and Sen (1970) have pointed out that transitivity may not be necessary for a social preference function. If the purpose of the latter is to select the most preferred social state, such a state could be reached by making the milder assumptions of *quasi-transitivity* or *acyclicity*. The relation (*R*) embodies indifference (*I*) as well as strict preference (*P*). Quasi-transitivity requires only that *APB*, *BPC* then *APC*. Under these conditions, *AIB* and *BIC* can occur along with *APC*. Society is indifferent between *A* and *B* but will choose *C*.

---

[2] For a somewhat different demonstration see Vickrey (1960).

[3] Transitivity implies the following: *APB*, *BPC* then *APC*; *APB*, *BIC* then *APC*; *AIB*, *BPC* then *APC*; *AIB*, *BIC* then *AIC*. *I* is indifference and *P* strict preference.

Given the same alternatives as the above if APB, BPC then *acyclicity* requires that *not CPA*. Since the relation CIA is not ruled out, the conditions for quasi-transitivity are not satisfied. If CPA then a cycling is generated. Higher taxes (A) are preferred to decreased defense expenditures (B), decreased defense expenditures (B) are preferred to reduced human services (C), yet reduced human services are preferred to higher taxes (A). Since the conditions of quasi-transitivity and acyclicity are less stringent than transitivity it was hoped they would have some advantages in deriving a social preference function. As it turns out, in a majority voting system to which we turn next, the advantages are rather minor. This is so because as Sen and Pattanaik (1969) show, the conditions for the minimal requirement of acyclicity are equivalent to the strict requirements of transitivity.

The Paradox of the Voting System

As far back as the eighteenth century, it was known that a majority voting system satisfies neither the transitivity or quasi-transitivity conditions. Assume three groups of equal number (1,2,3), three alternatives $(A,B,$ and $C)$, and an ordering relation of strict preference (P_i), where the subscript refers to a particular group. If AP_1B, BP_1C then AP_1C. If BP_2C, CP_2A then BP_2A. If CP_3A, AP_3B then CP_3B. A majority prefer A to B (groups 1 and 3) and B to C (1 and 2). Transitivity would imply society prefers A to C. Yet only group 1 has such a preference, and it does not represent a majority. As we mentioned in the last section, even the lesser requirement of acyclicity does not eliminate the paradox. Black (1948) showed that majority voting constitutes a well-behaved collective process if preferences are single-peaked and measurable along a single dimension.

In Figure 12.1 the three alternatives $(A,B,$ and $C)$ are measured along the horizontal axis and the utility (U_i) derived for each of these groups is measured vertically. For groups 1 and 2 there is a single peak in their ordering relation. In the first case the function declines after A while in the second, it increases to B, then declines. In contrast, in the third case the function peaks at A and C. These same results will occur not matter how the three options are listed along the horizontal axis. Collective preferences will never be transitive given this set of individual orderings. If we reorder the preferences of the third group as CP_3B, BP_3A, CP_3A, then we can represent them by the broken line in

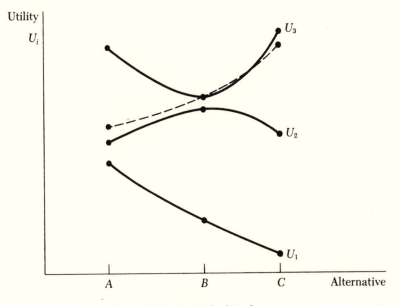

Figure 12.1   Individual Preferences

Figure 12.1. Now a majority prefer B to C and C to A and therefore B to A, thus satisfying the transitivity condition.

Unfortunately, in multidimensional cases even single-peaked preferences are insufficient to ensure transitivity; those choices considered Pareto optimal according to our earlier criteria may not be chosen in a majority voting system. Efforts to measure policy options in dollars or along a liberal conservative spectrum are sometimes attempts to convert multidimensional alternatives into a one-dimensional set.

Buchanan and Tullock (1962) explain the process of vote trading or "logrolling" as a device to arrive at consistent social preferences, but at the expense of what we earlier listed as condition 3. Assuming individual 1 is opposed to fluoridation of the water, he or she might agree to support individual 2's tax cap bill (about which 1 is indifferent) if 2 votes no on fluoridation. As a consequence, both are more likely to satisfy their preferences, but interdependencies among otherwise indifferent alternatives are introduced.

Condition 1 implies that the social welfare function be invariant for changes in tastes and preferences. Samuelson (1967) tries to render the problem more tractable by arguing that what is needed is a social ordering for a given set of choices not for every possible set. While appearing to simplify matters considerably, Ng (1980) demonstrates that even in such a situation Arrow's requirements cannot be met.

Although we have only been able to scratch the surface, clearly the issues involved in formulating a social welfare function are still in need of a great deal more research. Despite these problems, however, policy makers must measure societal preferences for what we called earlier public goods. The appropriate level and method of financing national defense is no less a real issue because of the above problems. In the next section we examine some recently derived methods for answering these and similar questions.

Preference Revelation

The voting system in any of its forms (majority rule, unanimity rule, plurality rule) differs fundamentally from the market system because of the absence of what some have called a *quid pro quo*. In the case of private goods, there is an exchange among individuals, but with public goods and social choices benefits are received without a direct payment. Because of this, it is difficult to determine individual preferences. In addition, individuals have an incentive to conceal their true feelings if by so doing they can reap the benefits of the good without bearing any of the cost.

Recent devices to measure social preferences have taken the form of imposing a *quid pro quo*. The Clarke-Groves tax, discussed earlier, imposes a tax on individuals if their vote is decisive but in an amount less than the benefits derived. The tax will prevent deception while at the same time ensure the Pareto optimal provision of the good. Since, however, the tax revenue represents a surplus, there is not Pareto optimality in a general equilibrium framework. In addition, the analysis assumes individuals can evaluate alternatives in terms of a common *numeraire*.

Table 12.1 gives the values placed on two alternatives A and B by four individuals. Assuming the assessment of preferences is accurate, A will be selected ($22 > 20$). Person 1 will pay a tax equal to the value of B (20) minus the value of A excluding person 1's assessment (12). Person 2 will analogously pay a tax equal to the value of B minus the value of A exclusive of person 2's assessment ($20 - 10$). Since the preferences of 3 and 4 do not affect the outcome, they do not pay.

By distorting true individual feelings in order to gain B, person 4

Table 12.1   Preferences and Clarke-Groves Taxes

| Voter | Value of Alternative | | Tax |
	A	B	
1	10	0	8
2	12	0	10
3	0	15	0
4	0	5	0
Total	22	20	

would have to affix a value greater than 7 so that the total value exceeds 22. By choosing 8, for example, person 4 will pay a tax equal to 7 (22 − 15) even though the true individual value is only 5. Although there is no incentive for individual deception, there is one for collusion and deception. If 3 or 4 collude and state preferences of 25 and 30, respectively, then *B* is chosen and neither pays a tax, since 22 − 30 and 22 − 25 are both negative.

In the Clarke-Groves tax the winners pay a tax equal to net loss of their vote on the other members of society. Such payments are not used in compensation of the losers, nor is it clear what effect such payments would have on the utility functions of the losers. Groves and Ledyard have proposed a variant of the above that results in the Pareto optimal decisions without the resultant surplus. Each individual acting independently is assumed to choose an increment to the public good that maximizes his or her net utility (that utility less tax). Taxes are set so that they just equal the cost of provision, and the level of production is optimal. If the rather simplistic independent action assumption is relaxed, then the results need not be Pareto optimal, and one wonders how decisions concerning increments in the public good could be made without considering others' views.

Mueller (1979) has suggested a "voting by veto" procedure whereby each participant can make one proposal and has the right to veto one proposal. Such a procedure assumes individuals are capable of making interpersonal utility evaluations in light of which a decision to veto is made. That proposal is finally settled on which is the collectively least objectionable. Like the others, Mueller's approach requires a *quid pro quo*, and also the ability of individuals to measure the costs and benefits of their own and in some cases the proposals of others.

Summary

The issue of social choice involves many aspects. In this chapter we examined whether a social welfare function existed and alternative devices for representing collective preferences. It is obvious that much of the precision and definitiveness that characterized our earlier discussion is lost. As yet, however, we have said nothing about the norms or criteria society should use in weighing individual preferences. This moves us even farther away from the realm of positive economics, although as we will see, having settled on criteria, their realization utilizes the techniques developed earlier.

References

Arrow, K. J. 1951. *Social Choice and Individual Values.* New York: Wiley.

Black, D. 1948. "On the Rationale of Group Decision Making." *Journal of Political Economy* 56:23–34.

Blau, J. H. 1957. "The Existence of Social Welfare Functions," *Econometrica* 25:302–13.

Buchanan, J. M., and G. Tullock. 1962. *The Calculus of Consent.* Ann Arbor: The University of Michigan Press.

Groves, T. and J. Ledyard. 1977. "Optimal Allocation of Public Goods: A Solution to the Free Rider Problem," *Econometrica* 45:783–809.

Mueller, D. C. 1979. *Public Choice.* Cambridge: Cambridge University Press.

Ng, Y.-K. 1980. *Welfare Economics.* New York: Halsted Press.

Plott, C. R. 1971. "Recent Results in the Theory of Voting." In M. D. Intriligator, ed. *Frontiers of Quantitative Economics.* Amsterdam: North-Holland.

Samuelson, P. A. 1967. "Arrow's Mathematical Politics." In S. Hook, ed. *Human Values and Economic Policy: A Symposium.* New York: New York University Press.

Sen, A. K. 1970. *Collective Choice and Social Welfare.* San Francisco: Holden-Day.

Sen, A. K., and P. K. Pattanaik. 1969. "Necessary and Sufficient Conditions for Rational Choice under Majority Decision." *Journal of Economic Theory* 1:178–202.

Vickrey, W. 1960. "Utility, Strategy, and Social Decision Rules." *Quarterly Journal of Economics* 74:507–35.

Supplementary Readings

Feldman, A. M. 1980. *Welfare Economics and Social Choice Theory.* Boston: Martinus Nijhoff Publishing.

Rawls, J. 1971. *A Theory of Justice.* Cambridge, Mass.: Harvard University Press.

Chapter 13

CRITERIA FOR SOCIAL DECISIONS

Many different operational criteria might be used in choosing alternative social states. In this chapter we introduce what may be thought of as the first and last such rules in the historical chain. These areas are as much the domain of social philosophers and political scientists as they are economists; thus we will see clearly the interdependencies between economics and the other social sciences. In its earliest historical stages economics was intimately linked to questions of justice and ethics. Though the twentieth century witnessed the growing influence of methodological techniques from mathematics and the natural sciences, the most basic questions to be asked of any economic system still concern the basic worth of mankind and the object of man's existence.

Classical Utilitarianism

In its simplest form the utilitarianism of Sidgwick, Pigou, Bentham, and Smith assumed utility that was both measurable and comparable.[1] Under such circumstances the social welfare curves could be depicted as in Figure 13.1a. Society would be *just* (i.e., in its best possible state) when the sum of the net utilities of its members was maximized. Utilitarianism extrapolates the principles of individual maximization to the collective. The distribution that maximizes total utility, is the one chosen. The distribution, however, does not initially enter as a constraint.

---

[1] For an excellent summary of utilitarianism see J. Rawls, *A Theory of Justice* (Cambridge: Belnap Press, 1971).

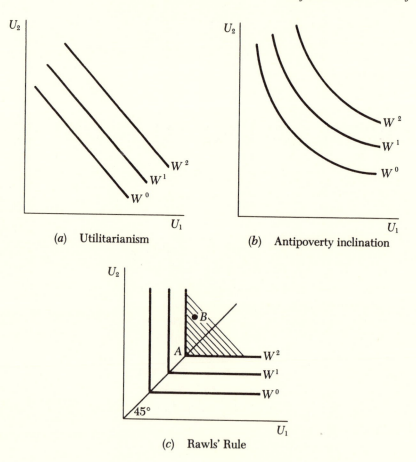

Figure 13.1   Social Welfare Contours

If we explicitly introduce distributional criteria, then the maximizing problem and the resultant indifference curves change. For example, the convex indifference curves in Figure 13.1*b* imply an antipoverty predisposition as evidenced by the declining rate of substitution. Along a curve, greater weight is given to the poor (those with lower utility).

Justice as Fairness

J. Rawls (1971) has proposed an alternative system of social justice and thereby decision making. Rawls begins by assuming that the members of society initially agree upon a principle ensuring each equal liberty or freedom outside the realm of economics. This decision is reached behind a "veil of ignorance" so that no one knows the implications of such an agreement on the distribution of income or wealth. In contrast to the utilitarian approach in which the focus is the "good," the first object in Rawls's theory is what is "right." Pursuit of the former is then undertaken within this social ordering ensuring individual rights. The distribution of income and wealth consequent upon social and economic institutions should be guided by what has come to be known as the "difference principle." This implies that any distribution of income (utility) that leads to greater equality is preferred unless both persons become better off. Policies are to be ordered in terms of the gains received by the least fortunate. As depicted in Figure 13.1c, social welfare curves would be right angles. Assuming an initial position at A, only those policies leading to points in the shaded area would be desirable. At B, inequality would increase (above the 45° line indicating a more favorable distribution for 2), but so also would the utility of 1. The policy would be judged by the gain to the latter, whose position is relatively worsened by the redistribution.

The best position occurs when the expectations of the worse off are maximized. No changes by the better off can improve the former's position. According to Rawls, this would be a perfectly *just* system. A *just* system (though not perfectly *just*) occurs when the better off contribute to the well-being of the less fortunate, so if the position of the better off declined, so would that of the worse off. The system is not perfectly *just* because increases by the better off would increase the well-being of the less fortunate.

Unfortunately, the Rawls criterion does not reconcile itself well with our earlier discussion of compensation criteria. Given a fixed income, Rawls would advocate an equal distribution, with each person getting an equal fraction of the total. When decisions must be made among alternative distribution, that one that realizes the greatest equality is chosen.

Despite the same measurement problems as discussed earlier being present, assume there are three policies (A,B,C) resulting in distributions of utility (income) to individuals 1, 2, and 3 as represented in Table 13.1. With Rawls's rule, B would be chosen over A and C. Relative to A, total well-being is greater with B, but between B and C it is less. Also, the gains to 2 and 3 (50 and 20, respectively) could more than compensate the loss to 1 (20) in choosing C over B (Kaldor criterion). On the other hand, the loser (1) could not bribe the other two

Table 13.1 Interpersonal Utility Distributions

	Distributions of Utility			
Alternative	1	2	3	Total
A	10	90	15	115
B	50	50	50	150
C	30	100	70	200

into not adopting the change (Hicks criterion). Finally, for any distribution of the total utilities (150) in *B*, we can find one with *C* that lies outside it, ensuring a utility possibility frontier everywhere farther from the origin (Samuelson criterion). Based on our earlier discussion, *C* would be the preferred option.

Until now we have assumed there was agreement on which individuals were better and worse off. In cases where there are many consumers and many commodities, evaluations of the better and worse off may differ, implying indecision regarding the appropriate policy.

Nozick's Critique

While no one would challenge the monumental contribution of Rawls, Nozick (1974) provides an excellent critical evaluation. He begins by questioning what the objective function is that Rawls is maximizing. Is it the sum of each individual's contribution or the sum of society's contribution, which, assuming cooperative behavior, would be greater. In addition, while the "difference principle" ensures support by the less well off, what motivates the better off to adhere to such a scheme? The following argument adopted from Nozick indicates some of the difficulties with the "difference principle."

Blue-collar workers have an annual income of $13,000, and professional workers have one of $20,000. Does this imply that the former are badly off because professionals are better off? Or that blue-collar workers suffer so that professionals benefit? Or that blue-collar workers would be better off if professionals were worse off? Or that the professionals' gain causes the blue-collar workers to suffer? The issue of the relations between the groups is never fully addressed, yet whether a tax scheme—for example, to increase the income of the worse off and reduce that of the better off—is implemented depends on just such a relation. Nozick finds particularly objectionable this absence of responsibility or what he calls "an entitlement or historical conception of distributive justice." Rawls begins by hypothesizing a system of justice without a system of entitlements. Initial endowments of individuals are viewed as pure gifts. In such a context the end result, the "end-state principle," is one of equality. Yet the right to such equality is never established. What is the foundation for such an individual entitlement?

Although Rawls's approach has received a great deal of attention, it is but one of many possible theories of fairness. Feldman and Kirman (1974) interpret fairness as "nonenvy." If given a group of individuals with utility functions U_i and vectors of commodities Y_i, $U_i(Y_i) \geqslant U_i(Y_j)$ for every i and j, then the allocation is *fair*. In other words, no one would prefer to be in anyone else's position. Unfortunately, nonenvy neither ensures the Pareto optimal result nor does the latter necessarily imply nonenvy.

Social Choice and the Distribution of Income

Society's collective preferences will determine which among the possible utility distributions is chosen. A utility possibilities curve (BB) is depicted in Figure 13.2. It differs from those drawn earlier in that it is

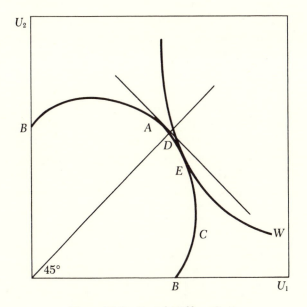

Figure 13.2   Social Welfare Optima

positively sloped as it approaches either axis. This implies interdependencies among utility functions so that increases in the utility of the worse off improve the utility of the best off as well. These positive segments are clearly not Pareto optimal. Classical utilitarianism as summarized in the Bentham social welfare function would lead us to maximize the sum of utilities. We will denote this by point A.[2] The effect such a policy has on income distribution depends on the utilities derived by each consumer. If consumer 2 derives three times as much utility from consumption of the same good as consumer 1, then 2 will end up with more utility (income) than 1. The more similar the individuals, the more compatible is the Bentham rule with equality. Rawls's approach would in this case lead us to C (i.e., the utility of the least well off $[U_1]$ would be maximized). Total utility is sacrificed in the interest of those having the least measured utility. In this particular case the difference principle is incompatible with utility equality shown at D, where the 45° line intersects the frontier. If, on the other hand, the frontier were negatively sloped throughout, Rawls's rule would ensure equality.

The convex social welfare contour (W) also gives preference to the person or group with the least utility. While we have deferred from specifying a functional form, Nash (1950) assumes the social welfare contour to be measured in the utility space as a rectangular hyperbole. The solution thus implies maximizing the product of individual utilities and is denoted E in Figure 13.2.[3] Although one can easily justify convexity of individual indifference curves in terms of the rate of commodity substitution, the same assumption at the collective level implies an egalitarian predisposition that cannot be demonstrated but only assumed.

The locus of utility combinations ensuring "nonenvy" may not lie on the utility possibilities curve at all. In Figure 13.3 we draw the indifference curves of consumers 1 and 2 relative to O_1 and O_2, respectively. Assuming a position such as A ensuring efficiency in consumption, we must now ask what would happen if the amount of Y_1 and Y_2 consumed by 1 were given to 2 and *vice versa*. A' is the mirror image

---

[2] Point A represents the tangency between the utility possibilities frontier and the farthest line from the origin, drawn perpendicular to the 45° line.

[3] As Ng points out, such an objective poses some serious problems, depending on the numeric values of the utilities. A welfare function of the form $W = W(U_1, U_2)$, where $U_1 = 1{,}000$ and $U_2 = 0$, would be rejected in favor of one where $U_1 = .5$ and $U_2 = 1$.

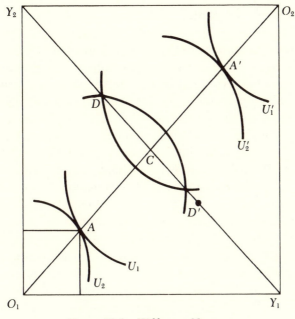

Figure 13.3   Welfare as Nonenvy

of A—that is, both points are equidistant on a straight line from the center of the box C. Clearly, consumer 1 would prefer A' since his utility is higher, and 2 would prefer A. Consumer 1 is envious of 2. Moving from a position D to D', on the other hand, implies the utilities of both decline so that D is a nonenvy point even though it does not ensure efficiency in consumption. The incompatibility of social welfare and efficiency poses a serious dilemma. It seems reasonable at this level of discussion at least to limit the set of feasible outcomes to those that are Pareto optimal.

The issues involved in the notion of *equity* and its embodiment in a social welfare function are extremely complex and complicated. Equal utility does not imply equality of income or vice versa, and equality of opportunity ensures neither. The evolution of thought in these areas requires the combined efforts of philosophers, theologians, and political scientists, as well as economists. The role of the economist predominates once these decisions have been reached and policies developed for their realization.

Locus of Decision Making

The literature on the processes for arriving at social choices is consider-able, but the appropriate governmental unit for implementing such decisions has yet to be carefully analyzed. An interesting discussion of the issues involved is found in the comments of J. Stein (1971) to the *Economic Report of the President, 1971.* The discussion centers on environmental quality, although it could be applied to many of the topics treated thus far. The conflict arises in that if the environment is a public good, optimality would require uniformity of costs and bene-fits. Yet the report supports local determination of environmental standards. This discussion is particularly appropriate given recent proposals for a *new federalism.* A similar analysis could be applied to a host of welfare programs whose benefits would vary among states.

In Figure 13.4 output (Y) is measured along the vertical axis, and pollution or environmental damage (X) is measured horizontally. It is further assumed that the latter is an input into the production of Y. As an example, steel production could be increased by allowing more pollution emittents. Region A places a higher price on pollution dam-age than region B. Assuming the production function is the same for

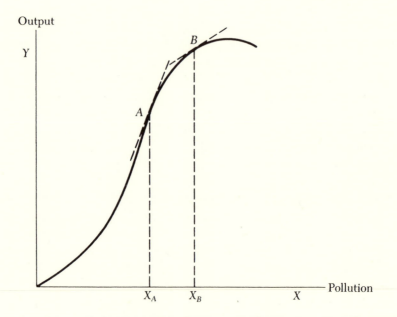

Figure 13.4   The Allocation of Pollution

both regions, individual efficiency would require that each equate the marginal physical product of pollution to its price. For a given set of prices (P_A and P_B), the resultant levels of pollution are denoted X_A and X_B, while the marginal physical products (MPP_A and MPP_B, respectively) are given by the slopes of the production function at A and B.

From a social perspective, it is clear a greater total output could be realized at the same level of total pollution. By reducing pollution one unit in B and increasing it one unit in A, output will change by $MPP_A - MPP_B$. A national policy establishing a single price for pollution is thus more socially efficient than disparate regional programs.

Other problems are associated with a regional approach as well. In the case of certain kinds of pollution, one locality may view an adjacent area as a *free good,* and attempt to use it as a dumping ground. When one area attempts to reduce pollution unilaterally, local industry often threatens to leave because of the resultant higher operational costs. The threatened industry loss may cause policy makers to ameliorate their efforts to limit pollution. Obviously, with a national policy such moves would not be profitable.

Another Apparent Dilemma

Much earlier we argued in favor of a dencentralized competitive market system in which individual decision making yielded Pareto optimality. In the competitive context we were critical of government policies that intruded on the market. From this earlier discussion, it would be easy to conclude that decentralization is preferable to any kind of national policy. The difference is, of course, in the nature of the goods being considered. While the competitive market is the optimal allocative tool for goods with clearly defined property rights, it breaks down when there are substantial externalities and the absence of such rights.

Much of the debate among policy makers centers on how to treat these nonprivate goods. On the one hand we could bypass the market by establishing government-mandated rules and regulations. As economists, however, we would prefer instead policies that internalize externalities and affix property rights to the environment via schemes such as environmental usage certificates. Such certificates could be sold at auction and could give the purchaser the right to discharge certain kinds and quantities of pollution into the environment. These entitlements alter the characteristics of the good and make it more like a private good, thereby allowing the market system to serve as the allocative tool. The auction process would establish a uniform price for pollution.

Summary

Our discussion of social choice theory has been quite cursory and superficial. We have focused on those aspects relevant to the implementation of optimizing policies. Despite the many problems in arriving at well-behaved collected preferences, policy makers must still make decisions affecting groups of people.

The ultimate constraint on the maximization of social welfare is the availability of natural resources in society. The finiteness of these factors will limit society's progress, and their misuse will work to the detriment of social well-being. The final chapter is devoted to this problem.

References

Feldman, A., and A. Kirman. 1974. "Fairness and Envy." *American Economic Review* 64:995–1005.

Nash, J. 1950. "The Bargaining Problem." *Econometrica* 18:115–62.

Nozick, R. 1974. *Anarchy, State and Utopia.* New York: Basic Books.

Rawls, J. 1971. *A Theory of Justice.* Cambridge, Mass.: Belnap Press.

Stein, J. 1971. "Micro-Economic Aspects of Public Policy." *The American Economic Review* 61:531–37.

U.S. Council of Economic Advisors. 1971. *Economic Report of the President.* Washington D.C.: Govt. Printing Office.

Chapter 14

SOCIAL WELFARE AND NATURAL RESOURCE USE

It should be clear that the constraints on the realization of societal objectives are not adequately handled in an analysis of individual decision-making units. Natural resources such as air, water, and energy are generally thought to be limitless in supply by individuals, but for society they are finite and often nonrenewable. The issue society then confronts is how best to employ these resources to maximize welfare over time.

In many respects such resources represent the ultimate limitations on welfare because the effects of inappropriate, nonoptimal use often cannot be corrected or reversed. The first issue we must address, then, is how best to allocate such resources. Although much of the concern over natural resources is relatively recent, Harold Hotelling (1931) set forth the basics of the economic analysis back in 1931.

Entropy

The first law of thermodynamics postulates that energy is neither created nor destroyed in a chemical reaction. Therefore, the use of oil and natural gas to turn the wheels of industry does not lessen the energy content of the heat and power generated. What does occur is a conversion from energy in a form over which many has control—that is, "free" or low-entropy energy is converted into a more dissipated, chaotic form referred to as high-entropy or "bound" energy.

The second law of thermodynamics (entropy law) states that the bound or uncontrollable energy of a closed system continuously increases so that order turns into disorder. Economic development has proceeded by utilizing low-entropy energy, and, coupled with the second law of thermodynamics, the result has been the dissipation of free energy. Low-entropy energy sources may be either stocks or flows. Mineral and terrestrial deposits constitute the former while solar radiation and wind velocity are flow sources. Since stocks are more easily harnessed, they have until now been employed to the greatest degree. One of the implications of the entropy law is that recycling can never be the ultimate answer to the finiteness of nonrenewable resources since the recoverability of any resource will dissipate with use.

The discussion of natural resources engenders consideration of many of the issues discussed earlier. Some natural resources are appropriable while for others exclusion is very difficult. Appropriability is contingent on property rights and tends to exist for forests and mines but not for water and the environment. The absence of total appropriability implies the presence of externalities in either the production or consumption of many resources. A final issue in the treatment of natural resources is renewability. With sufficient time fisheries and timber can be replenished; however, it is becoming increasingly evident that the supply of oil and precious metals is finite and nonrenewable. In our discussion we will use both comparative static and dynamic approaches beginning with renewable resources. Our point of departure is a model originally developed by V. L. Smith (1968).

Comparative Statics—Renewable Resources

In the case of resources such as fish, timber, humans, and so on, one must consider the biologically determined rate of growth. Assume the resource (x) grows at a rate that is a function (f) of its size:

$$\overset{o}{x} = \frac{dx}{dt} = f(x). \tag{14.1}$$

The function f is assumed to have an inverted U form indicating a minimum $(x_{\min})$ and maximum $(x_{\max})$ sustaining population. Smaller or larger populations will lead to negative growth rates. The function f represents the combined effects of births, deaths, and growth. The relationship between stock size and growth is depicted in Figure 14.1, where x' is the stock size producing the largest growth rate or the maximum sustainable yield.

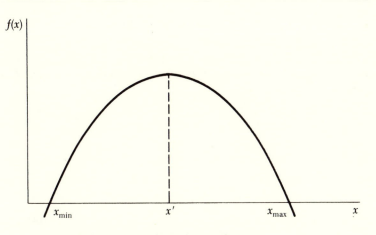

Figure 14.1   Biological Growth Curve

Man enters the picture as a predator that uses x at a rate of $\mathbf{x}$ per unit of capital or per firm. Letting K denote the total homogeneous units of capital, the growth in x will then be:

$$\overset{o}{x} = f(x) - K\mathbf{x}. \qquad (14.2)$$

Obviously, in the case of nonrenewable resources $f(x)$ will be identically zero.

Costs

It will be assumed that cost per firm (c) is an increasing function of the firm's output $(\mathbf{x})$. In addition, for many resources it may be reasonable to assume costs are inversely related to the stock. For fish and timber, for example, cost will tend to decrease, the larger the stock and increase, the greater the harvest rate.

Costs are also likely to be affected by the number of predators. The larger the size of the exploiting industry, the higher the costs to an individual firm. The larger the number of fishing boats, the higher the costs to any individual fisherman. This may be considered a "crowding" externality. We can write the cost function as:

$$c = \phi(\mathbf{x},x,K), \qquad (14.3)$$

where

$$\frac{\partial c}{\partial x} > 0, \qquad \frac{\partial c}{\partial x} \leq 0, \qquad \frac{\partial c}{\partial K} \geq 0.$$

Assuming pure competition in the product market with price P, total industry revenue will be:

$$PKx. \tag{14.4}$$

Profit per unit (π) will then be:

$$\pi = Px - \phi(x,x,K). \tag{14.5}$$

The firm's first-order profit-maximizing condition with respect to the decision variable x is then:

$$P - \frac{\partial \phi}{\partial x} = 0, \tag{14.6}$$

or price equals marginal cost.

Given the same cost and revenue functions as above, but allowing for freedom of entry and exit, new firms will enter when profits are positive and depart or be driven out when they are negative. This can be expressed as:

$$\overset{o}{K} = \delta[Px - \phi(x,x,K)], \qquad \delta > 0, \tag{14.7}$$

where δ is the rate of adjustment of the industry to the presence of profits.

Equations (14.2) and (14.7), along with initial values of x and K, form a first-order differential equation system, which may be rewritten as:

$$\overset{o}{x} = F(x,K), \tag{14.8}$$

$$\overset{o}{K} = I(x,K). \tag{14.9}$$

From (14.8) and (14.9) one can map the locus of industry sizes (K) and resource supplies (x) consistent with equilibrium in the size of the exploiting industry $(\overset{o}{K} = 0)$ and the maintenance of a fixed resource supply $(\overset{o}{x} = 0)$. Some illustrative schedules are portrayed in Figure 14.2, where the points P^* and P^{**} represent static general equilibria, where $F(x,K) = I(x,K) = 0$.

Depending on the values of K and x, five different responses to a disequilibrium are discernible. The direction of the arrows in Figure 14.2 indicates the behavior of the industry and resource stock. In region *A*, for example, stock use exceeds its renewal rate so that *x* declines and industry size is excessive, leading to rising costs and the exodus of firms. Just the opposite occurs in *D*. Without knowing the specific location of the system, it is not possible to say whether it will move toward an equilibrium: which of the equilibria is preferred depends on social priorities. This in turn involves us in a discussion of society's time horizon: the greater the weight given to the preferences of future generations, the smaller the rate of exploitation of current supplies.

The Effects of Nonappropriability

In the previous discussion we assumed a common property resource so that firms in the industry could not prevent sharing their profits with new entrants—that is, they could not internalize the profits associated with this resource. Had a contract existed giving a particular firm or firms exclusive or ownership rights to the resource, the entry of other firms could have been prevented. The extent of property rights will have important implications for the characteristics of the industry.

Consider an example used by S. Cheung (1970) to examine the

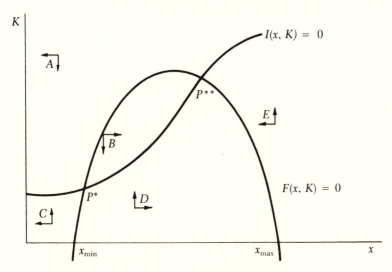

Figure 14.2   Dynamic Equilibria

fishing industry. At one extreme we will assume a single fisherman with exclusive rights to a particular fishing reserve. With a single variable (labor) production function, profit maximization will occur where the marginal physical product of labor (MPP_1) is equal to the real wage (w). The maximizing input of labor is denoted by L_1 in Figure 14.3. The difference between the average product of labor (AP) and the marginal product measures the rent consequent upon the possession of property rights. It is denoted by AB in Figure 14.3. If we drop the assumption of appropriability, then the rent will induce other firms to enter. The marginal product of the second firm (MPP_2) will begin at point B. The marginal productivity of labor in the second firm will begin at the average industry productivity, and firm 2 will hire labor up to L_2. The process will continue until all the rent is eliminated and the average productivity is equal to the real wage at L_4.

The adjustment process is a bit more complicated than that portrayed above, however. When firm 2 enters, the marginal productivity of firm 1 is adversely affected. At a level of total employment L_2, the

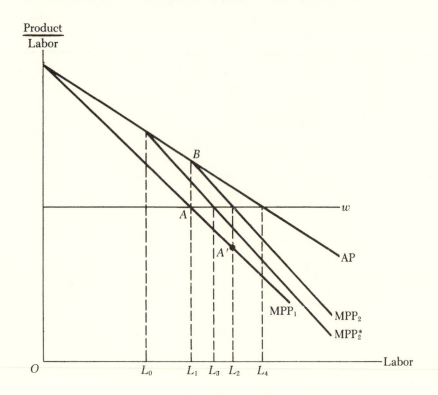

Figure 14.3   Labor Productivity in Fishing

marginal physical productivity of 1 is A' less than the real wage w. Firm 1 will reduce employment from L_1 to L_0 or until the marginal productivity of the last worker in the industry equals w. Finally, the reduction of employment in 1 alters the productivity in 2 as evidenced by MPP$_2^*$. The long-run implications are that the fishing industry should consist of a very large number of very small firms with no above-normal profits.

Many factors may limit or retard the adjustment process we have described. For example, either natural or artificial barriers to entry may exist. Additionally production costs need not be identical among all firms. Despite these qualifications, however, one has to look no farther than New Bedford and Gloucester along the eastern coast of Massachusetts to see an industry consisting primarily of many very small firms that are using relatively small boats and earning not much more than a break-even level of income. Efforts to exclude foreign fishing vessels and limit the catch are similarly consistent.

Dynamics

Particularly in the case of nonrenewable resources, we must consider the time horizon over which we intend to maximize. Our discussion will begin with renewable resources and conclude with the nonrenewable case. The same symbols will be used as previously, but now they will be dated. The goal of the firm is now to maximize the discounted present value (DPV) of the flow of profit derived from harvesting a resource stock. Assuming that costs are determined by the harvest $(\mathbf{x}_t)$ and the stock x_t, that the cost function is invariant over time, and that there is pure competition in the product market, the objective to be maximized, may be expressed as:

$$\text{DPV} = \frac{P_1\mathbf{x}_1 - C(\mathbf{x}_1,x_1)}{(1+i)} + \ldots + \frac{P_T\mathbf{x}_T - C(\mathbf{x}_T,x_T)}{(1+i)^T}, \qquad (14.10)$$

where $t = 1, \ldots, T$.

This discrete formulation of the maximizing problem is quite common in economics, and the interested reader may consult Quirk (1976). The first-order maximizing condition may be derived intuitively in the following way. A change in the catch rate $(\mathbf{x}_t)$ has both an immediate impact and a future or deferred effect. In the first period the effect will be the difference between price and marginal cost times the change in the harvest:

$$(P_1 - MC_1)\,\Delta x_1.$$

An increase in x_1 decreases the subsequent stock, leading to an increase in cost in period 2:

$$\frac{\partial C}{\partial x_2}\,\Delta x_1.$$

Finally, assuming harvests in periods subsequent to the second are unchanged, the harvest in period 2 must change by Δx_1 plus the effect that a change in x_1 has on the biological growth rate (df/dx):

$$\Delta x_2 = \left(1 + \frac{df}{dx_2}\right)\Delta x_1.$$

The change in profits in period 2 will then be:

$$(P_2 - MC_2)\left(1 + \frac{df}{dx_2}\right)\Delta x_1 - \partial C/\partial x_2\,\Delta x_1.$$

Discounting and setting the first derivative equal to zero yields (where i is the interest rate):

$$\frac{P_1 - MC_1}{(1 + i)} - \frac{(P_2 - MC_2)\left(1 + \dfrac{df}{dx_2}\right) - \partial C/\partial x_2}{(1 + i)^2} = 0. \qquad (14.11)$$

If for the moment we assume that cost, price, and harvest are the same each year, the above can be rewritten as:

$$P - MC - \left(\frac{-\partial C/\partial x}{i - df/dx}\right) = 0. \qquad (14.12)$$

To the direct effect associated with harvesting (MC) must be added the subsequent effect on cost due to changes in the stock $(\partial C/\partial x)$; the latter is discounted by the interest less the biological growth rate. The additional cost will be positive as long as the interest rate exceeds the growth rate.

In the absence of appropriability, future profits will be sacrificed for immediate gains since firms have no assurance that future gains will not be taken by someone else. This myopia will lead firms to ignore both the interest rate and the stock cost $(\partial C/\partial x)$. Rewriting (14.12), we can show more clearly the relation between the biological growth rate and the firm's profitability:

$$\frac{df}{dx} = i - \frac{\partial C/\partial x}{MC - P}.$$

Although many possible solutions may exist, in Figure 14.4 we show a profit-maximizing position at A where the slope of the biological growth curve equals that of the isoprofit line π. In the absence of appropriability profits would lead to the entry of competitors so that in the long run we would be at a position such as B where profits are zero. The isoprofit line π' is drawn more steeply than π to indicate the failure to consider i and $\partial C/\partial x$. It should be obvious that the same harvest as at B could be achieved at C but with a larger stock $x_C > x_D$, and, therefore, at a lower cost.

In cases where transaction costs render appropriability infeasible, such as in the preservation of certain species of wild life, the government has often assumed control of the resource. The criteria pursued is generally that of maintaining that stock x_D that maximizes harvest. By ignoring harvest costs, policy makers would maintain a stock less than consistent with profit maximization.

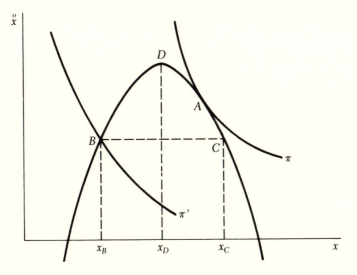

Figure 14.4   Equilibria with Renewable Resources

Nonrenewability

In the case of a nonrenewable resource, the stock diminishes by the amount of the harvest:

$$x_{t+1} = x_t - \mathbf{x}_t. \tag{14.13}$$

An increase in the harvest in period t ($\Delta \mathbf{x}_t$) will increase current profits by:

$$(P_t - MC_t)\Delta \mathbf{x}_t. \tag{14.14}$$

Assuming the harvest in the next time period is reduced by $\Delta \mathbf{x}_t$ so that subsequent harvests are unaffected, subsequent profits will fall by:

$$[P_{t+1} - (MC_{t+1} - \partial C/\partial x_{t+1})]\Delta \mathbf{x}_t. \tag{14.15}$$

Setting the discounted values to zero and rewriting yields:

$$P_{t+1} - P_t(1 + i) = MC_{t+1} - [MC_t(1 + i) + \partial C/\partial x_{t+1}]. \tag{14.16}$$

Increases in the interest rate raise prices, implying a more rapid exploitation of the stock in the present. High interest rates increase the opportunity cost associated with maintaining a resource stock. As a consequence the interest rate has important implications for intertemporal societal preferences. Hypermetropic societies will benefit from low interest rates since they imply less rapid resource utilization and relatively large future supplies. High interest favor the more myopic.

As we mentioned in our discussion of optimality over time, it has often been argued that, since there isn't a market where future generations can express their preferences, the appropriate discount factor (interest rate) in public policy decisions regarding the use of natural resources should be set lower than the private rate. Such a policy would lead to greater conservation of the resource, while at the same time lessen any negative externalities associated with rapid exhaustion. Thus far we have ignored the externality problem, but clearly the issue of externalities is intimately bound up with that of natural resources.

"Hotelling Rule"

We began our discussion by mentioning a seminal article by H. Hotelling. One of the implications of his analysis has come to be called

"Hotelling's Rule," and it follows naturally from equation 14.16. The net price of an exhaustible resource must increase at a rate equal to the interest rate to ensure efficiency in extraction in a competitive market. In the continuous case

$$P_t = P_0 \, e^{it},$$

where P_t is the net price in period t, P_0 is the initial price and i the rate of interest. Net price refers to market price minus marginal extraction cost.

In the case of a monopolist, marginal revenue—and not net price—will grow at a rate i. Hotelling believed that under monopoly price would rise less rapidly and depletion occur less quickly than with competition. Subsequent writers have shown this to be the case as long as the elasticity of demand decreases as quantity increases.

Summary

The topic of natural resources brings together many of the issues involved in the treatment of welfare economics. For many resources, property rights either do not exist or are difficult to delineate so that a competitive market system will not ensure efficient utilization. Additional issues arise concerning the time horizon for the optimizing process and the weights to be affixed to the future. The market rate of interest may be a poor index of the social discount rate because of its bias in favor of current generations. We must then examine how to assess the collective social preference and choose policies consistent with it. Again we are led back to the same questions with which we began: What is the objective (equity)? and What are the conditions to best achieve it (efficiency)?

References

Cheung, S. 1970. "The Structure of a Contract and the Theory of a Non-Exclusive Resource." *Journal of Law and Economics* 13:49–70.

Hotelling, H. 1931. "The Economics of Exhaustible Resources." *Journal of Political Economy* 39:137–75.

Quirk, J. P. 1976. *Intermediate Microeconomics*. Chicago: Science Research Associates.

Smith, V. 1968. "Economics of Production from Natural Resources." *American Economic Review* 58:407–31.

Supplementary Readings

Devarajan, S., and A. C. Fisher. 1981. "Hotelling's 'Economics of Exhaustible Resources': Fifty Years Later." *Journal of Economic Literature* 19:65–73.

Solow, R. M. 1974. "The Economics of Resources or the Resources of Economics." *American Economic Review* 64:1–14.

EPILOGUE

A natural tendency in debate is to make a point by polarizing, often with the use of hyperbole. Political parties and their representatives are often classified as being for "big business" or for the "working class." The former implies less government intervention, a greater reliance on the market system, and an emphasis on efficiency, while the latter is more interventionist, particularly with regard to income redistribution (equity). To a degree one can view the liberal-conservative debate as hinging on the weights to be affixed to the goals of efficiency and equity. It is important, therefore, that one clearly understands the origin and interpretation of these terms, as well as their complementarity and substitutability.

The object of welfare economics is to define the terms "efficiency" and "equity" and then develop criteria for their realization. We began by using the techniques developed for individual decision-making economic agents and then attempted to generalize to society as a whole. Although the criteria for achieving an objective are quite similar, whether at the individual or collective level, there is much less consensus over the formulation of objectives. In contrast to individual choice, where consumers maximize utility and firms profit, there is considerable controversy over whether a social welfare function can be derived and, if it can, what its objective is.

Methods of arriving at society's preferences for nonmarket goods involve economics with many other disciplines (political science, moral theology, and so on). This growing area of research is labeled "social choice theory," and, while it is true these same issues motivate much of the early welfare economics of Bentham and Sidgwick, it is now thought of as separate though not distinct. The potential for economics would appear greatest in the derivation of optimizing conditions rather than objective formulation. We have tried to show the effects of the market system in both its pure form and with distortions (imperfect competition, externalities, public goods). In the latter cases we have

185

discussed policies to achieve the first-best results, and, where this is impossible, second-best solutions.

The finiteness of natural resources has become ever more obvious. In light of this it is essential that consideration be given to the conditions for optimizing over time. While to any individual economic agent resources may be potentially limitless, for society these same finite resources must be used in ways that ensure the well-being of both current and future generations. Again, the issue of weighing individual and group preferences arises, but now decisions must also be made regarding intergenerational priorities. Natural resources constitute the ultimate constraint on the achievement of societal objectives. Optimal depletion strategies require both efficiency in utilization and equity in intertemporal distribution. Concepts such as compensation criteria take on new and challenging dimensions when viewed in terms of winners and losers over time.

This concludes our discussion of the issues involved in social decision making. Despite the vast amount of research already completed, many unsettled issues still remain. And although one can feel a reasonable degree of confidence in the application of maximum principles, a great deal has yet to be done with the techniques for formulating social objectives.

Appendix

MATHEMATICAL REVIEW

Here we review some mathematical concepts that should be familiar to most students with a year's course in calculus. What may not be apparent, even to those with extensive backgrounds in mathematics, is the application of these techniques to economics. Rather than methods of solution, our discussion will concentrate on the intuitive applicability of mathematics to economic analysis.

Single-Variable Functions

Assume a continuous functional relationship between two variables y and x of the form:

$$y = f(x). \tag{A.1}$$

The derivative of y with respect to x, dy/dx, is the rate of change in y given an infinitesimal change in x.

The Derivative

Given an arbitrary increment in x, say Δx, the resultant value of y will be:

$$y + \Delta y = f(x + \Delta x). \tag{A.2}$$

Bringing y over to the right-hand side and dividing both sides by Δx gives:

$$\frac{\Delta y}{\Delta x} = \frac{f(x + \Delta x) - f(x)}{\Delta x}. \tag{A.3}$$

The derivative of y with respect of x, dy/dx, is the ratio of the change in y to the change in x as the latter (Δx) approaches zero, or:

$$\frac{dy}{dx} = \lim_{\Delta x \to 0} \frac{\Delta y}{\Delta x} = \lim_{\Delta x \to 0} \frac{f(x + \Delta x) - f(x)}{\Delta x}. \tag{A.4}$$

Geometrically, the derivative of a function at a point is the slope of the tangent line to the curve at that point. Finding derivatives is called differentiation. With reference to (A.1), dy/dx is sometimes referred to as the first-order derivative. Higher-order derivatives are obtained by repeated differentiation of (A.1). The second-order derivative is obtained by differentiating (A.1) twice. What we are doing then is taking the derivative of the first-order derivative $[d(dy/dx)/dx]$, or, expressed more simply, d^2y/dx^2. The nth-order derivative will then be denoted d^ny/dx^n. Sometimes first-order derivatives are denoted f' and second-order derivatives f''.

Continuity and Differentiability

A function $y = f(x)$ is continuous at x^0 if (1) x^0 is in the domain of the function, (2) the limit of $f(x)$ as x approaches x^0 exists, and (3) the limit of $f(x)$ as x approaches x^0 is equal to $f(x^0)$. A function is said to be continuous if it is continuous at every point in the domain of x. If a function can be differentiated, then it is continuous. However, the converse need not be the case: continuity does not imply differentiability. Even though a function is continuous, the difference quotient need not have a limit.

To illustrate, consider the function $y = |x - 3| + 1$ defined for all real values of x. The function is continuous at $x = 3$ since (1) $x = 3$ is in the domain of the function, (2) the limit of y as x approaches 3 exists, and (3) the limit is equal to y at $x = 3$ $[f(3) = 1]$.

Differentiability requires the limit of the difference quotient as x approaches 3 exists:

$$\lim_{x \to 3} \frac{f(x) - f(3)}{x - 3} = \lim_{x \to 3} \frac{|x - 3| + 1 - 1}{x - 3} = \lim_{x \to 3} \frac{|x - 3|}{x - 3}.$$

In this case it does not exist since the left- and right-side limits are not equal. Considering the right-side limit, x must exceed 3, therefore:

$$\lim_{x \to 3^+} \frac{|x - 3|}{x - 3} = \lim_{x \to 3^+} \frac{x - 3}{x - 3} = 1.$$

In the left-side limit, x must be less than 3; thus:

$$\lim_{x \to 3^-} \frac{|x - 3|}{x - 3} = \lim_{x \to 3^-} \frac{-(x - 3)}{x - 3} = -1.$$

On your own, you should plot this function to see graphically what nondifferentiability implies. Most functions in economics are assumed continuous and differentiable.

Maxima and Minima

If the derivative is positive, the value of y will increase; if it is negative, y will decrease. When the derivative is equal to zero, a maximum, minimum, or point of inflexion will occur.[1] With any of these cases, the tangent line will be horizontal.

The *necessary* condition for an extremum (a maximum or minimum) is that the first derivative equal zero. This is frequently referred to as the *first-order* condition. To be certain we have an extremum and not an inflexion point, we must consider the *sufficient* or *second-order* conditions. For a maximum, the second-order derivative (d^2y/dx^2) must be negative, and for a minimum it must be positive. The second-order derivative gives indication of the direction in which the function is moving.

If the first derivative is zero for some value of x (say x^0), and the second derivative is negative (positive), this implies that incrementing x in the neighborhood of x^0 will cause $f(x)$ to decline (increase). In most of the text we consider only the first-order conditions, assuming the second-order conditions are satisfied.

Multivariable Functions

It may be that y is not determined by a single variable x but by a number of determinants $(x_1, x_2, \ldots, x_n)$. The functional relationship now takes the form:

$$y = f(x_1, \ldots, x_n). \tag{A.4}$$

We may want to find how y changes given a change in one of the

---

[1] At a point of inflexion the function crosses the horizontal tangent line.

determinants (x_i) holding all others constant. This is called the partial derivative of y with respect to x_i and may be denoted $\partial y/\partial x_i$. Alternatively, it may be expressed as f_i', where the subscript indicates the variable with respect to which the differentiation is done. Incrementing x_i by Δx_i, holding all other determinants constant, and proceeding as we did above, the partial derivative can be defined more precisely as:

$$\frac{\partial y}{\partial x_i} = \lim_{\Delta x_i \to 0} \frac{f(x_1, \ldots, x_{i-1}, x_i + \Delta x_i, x_{i+1}, \ldots, x_n) -}{\Delta x_i}$$

$$\frac{f(x_1, \ldots, x_{i-1}, x_i, x_{i+1}, \ldots, x_n)}{\Delta x_i} \quad (A.5)$$

Continuity and differentiability are defined analogously to the single-variable case.

Maxima and Minima

When all the partial derivatives are equal to zero,

$$\frac{\partial y}{\partial x_i} = 0 \qquad (i = 1, \ldots, n), \tag{A.6}$$

the function will attain a maximum, minimum, or saddle point.[2] Equation (A.6) is the necessary or first-order condition for an extremum in the multivariable case.

In the same way we can talk about higher-order derivatives, we can also consider higher-order partial derivatives. The second-order partial of x_i with respect to y is denoted $\partial^2 y/\partial x^2_i$ or $\partial(\partial y/\partial x_i)/\partial x_i$. We can also find cross-partials such as $\partial^2 y/\partial x_i \partial x_j$ $(i \neq j)$. Using an alternative notation, the above may be represented as $f_{x_i x_i}$ and $f_{x_i x_j}$.

The sufficient or second-order conditions in the multivariable case are more difficult to derive. What we are concerned with doing, however, is checking that the function reaches an extremum for movements in all directions—that is, for changes in all the determinants. Table A.1 opposite gives the first- and second-order conditions for the two-variable case; this will suffice for all purposes.

---

[2] A saddle point occurs when, for a particular x_i or set of x_is, y is at a minimum (maximum), while for another x_j $(i \neq j)$ or set of x_js, it is at a maximum (minimum).

Table A.1 Extremum Conditions for $y = f(x_1, x_2)$

Conditions	Maximum	Minimum
First-order (necessary)	$f_{x_1} = f_{x_2} = 0$	$f_{x_1} = f_{x_2} = 0$
Second-order (sufficient)	$f_{x_1 x_1}, f_{x_2 x_2} < 0$ and $f_{x_1 x_1} f_{x_2 x_2} > f_{x_1 x_2}^2$	$f_{x_1 x_1}, f_{x_2 x_2} > 0$ and $f_{x_1 x_1} f_{x_2 x_2} > f_{x_1 x_2}^2$

Maximization Subject to Constraints

Most problems in economics involve finding an extremum subject to certain side conditions or constraints. A number of different mathematical methods can be used in such problems; however, we will focus on the technique of Lagrange. Our discussion will concentrate on a two-variable case, though generalization to larger dimensions is quite straightforward. Assume we want to find the extremum of $y = f(x_1, x_2)$ subject to a constraint of the form $z = g(x_1, x_2)$. We can form a new function w that includes both the objective function and the constraint stated in implicit form (i.e., in a form that makes it equal to zero):

$$w = f(x_1, x_2) + \lambda[g(x_1, x_2) - z]. \tag{A.7}$$

The term λ is called the Lagrangian multiplier. The first-order conditions for an extremum of (A.7) are that the first-order partials with respect to x_1, x_2 and λ equal zero:

$$\frac{\partial w}{\partial x_1} = f_1 + \lambda g_1 = 0, \tag{A.8}$$

$$\frac{\partial w}{\partial x_2} = f_2 + \lambda g_2 = 0, \tag{A.9}$$

$$\frac{\partial w}{\partial \lambda} = g(x_1, x_2) - z = 0. \tag{A.10}$$

From equations (A.8), (A.9), and (A.10) it may be possible to solve for the values of x_1, x_2, and λ that satisfy the first-order conditions. The Lagrangian multiplier (λ) measures the effect on the objective function of a marginal relaxation of the constraint or auxiliary relation.

The second-order conditions for an extremum are quite involved and will not be discussed here. In the text, it is assumed the functions are well behaved so that satisfying the first-order conditions ensures meeting the sufficient (second-order) conditions.

Concavity and Convexity

Generally in the context of extremal problems, functions are well behaved if they satisfy certain conditions with respect to concavity. A function $f(x)$ is concave if:

$$f[\Theta x + (1 - \Theta) x^0] \geq \Theta f(x) + (1 + \Theta)f(x^0) \qquad \text{for } 0 \leq \Theta \leq 1. \quad \text{(A.11)}$$

If the function f is differentiable, the condition may be expressed as:

$$f(x) \leq f(x^0) + \partial f/\partial x \big|_{x^0} (x - x^0). \qquad \text{(A.12)}$$

The last term in (A.12) refers to the partial of f with respect to x evaluated at x^0. Figures A.1 and A.2 satisfy the conditions for concavity according to (A.11) and (A.12), respectively. If the inequalities in the definitions are reversed, then $f(x)$ is a *convex* function.

A *quasi-concave* function is one such that $(1) f(x) \geq f(x^0)$ implies $f[\Theta x + (1 - \Theta)x^0] \geq f(x^0)$ for $0 \leq \Theta \leq 1$, or $(2) f(x) \geq f(x^0)$ implies $(\partial f/\partial x) \big|_{x^0} (x - x^0) \geq 0$ if $f(x)$ is differentiable. Clearly, all concave functions are quasi-concave. For the single-variable case, a convex function is also quasi-concave.

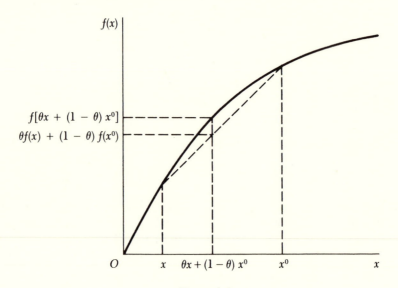

Figure A.1

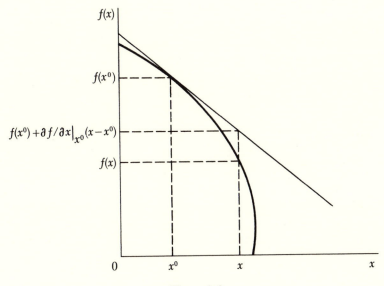

Figure A.2

A function quasi-concave over some domain need not be outside this domain. The function $f(x_1, x_2) = x_1, x_2$ is quasi-concave for x_1 and $x_2 \geq 0$ but not for negative values of x_1 and x_2. For a quasi-concave function, if $\partial f / \partial x_i \geq 0$ and $x_i \geq 0$, the isovalue curves must be convex to the origin. If $\partial f / \partial x_i \leq 0$ and $x_i \geq 0$, the isovalue curves are concave to the origin. This is the usual assumption in deriving indifference curves and production-possibility frontiers in economics. For the two-variable case, two illustrations of quasi-concave functions are given in Figures A.3 and A.4 (where x refers to x_1, x_2 and c is a constant).

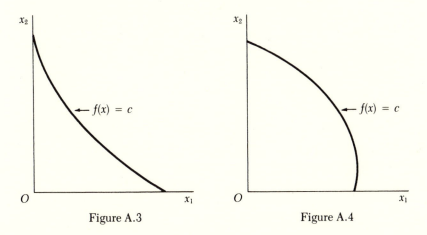

Figure A.3   Figure A.4

INDEX